ANDREA
PIRLO

WITH ALESSANDRO ALCIATO

I THINK THEREFORE I PLAY

translated from the Italian
by Mark Palmer

BackPage Press

For my family, my wife and my children.
A simple dedication for special people
Andrea Pirlo

For Niccolò – because every day is Christmas
Alessandro Alciato

CONTENTS

Introduction

By Cesare Prandelli, Italy manager

Andrea Pirlo is a player who belongs to everyone. Guys like him should be a protected species. Every ground is Andrea's ground – fans look at him and see a universal champion, capable of taking them beyond the concept of supporting a single team. They see Italy.

Truth be told, it wouldn't surprise me if Andrea went to bed at night wearing blue pyjamas, the same colour as the *Azzurri* jersey. His love for that shirt is immense; absolutely boundless.

Before speaking about the Andrea of today (and tomorrow, and forever), we need to go back to the days when I coached the Atalanta youth teams. My responsibility was the *Allievi*[1], and during the week there was always a lot of chat about the toughest opponents and most exciting young talents we'd come up against over the season. Naturally we'd reference Milan and Inter, but most of all we'd talk about Brescia. That rivalry was all about local pride.

As we prepared for training one day, one of my assistants burst into the changing room completely out of breath.

"Cesare, I've seen a really talented kid. Insanely good. Trouble is, he plays for the Brescia *Giovanissimi*[2]."

What struck me wasn't so much what he'd said, rather the incredulous look on his face. This was a guy who'd watched hundreds of games in his time. As luck would have it, the following week Atalanta *Giovanissimi* were down to play that self-same Brescia team. A side where a slight little kid two or three years younger than his team-mates was bobbing and weaving his way round the pitch. That kid's name was Pirlo.

He left me speechless. I'd never seen anything like it. I got the distinct impression that everyone was watching him and him alone, thinking the exact same thing: "This is the one. This is *the* new talent." In the eyes of others, he's never been a child.

Pirlo brings people together because he *is* football. He's the most skilful type of player, someone who's never done anything horribly wrong – he's the essence of the game. For that reason, he's recognised as a global talent, a player who sends out a positive message with every touch he takes. The message is that sometimes even normal guys can be truly exceptional.

Those of us lucky enough to be in Bergamo that day bore witness to his ability. On the pitch, he goes about his business with a disarming nonchalance. Few and far between are the players even capable of conceiving of some of the things he does. It's no surprise that at the end of every Italy game, there's a queue of opposition players outside our dressing room wanting to swap shirts with him. They like him, too.

The really extraordinary thing is that Andrea is a silent leader – something that's not easy to find in the world of football. Back in my playing days, before I became a coach,

I got to know a fantastic man, Gaetano Scirea[3]. It's uncanny how closely Andrea resembles him. Their way of conducting themselves is identical. On the rare occasions when these silent leaders choose to say something, the rest of the dressing room shuts up and listens.

I've witnessed this first-hand on a couple of memorable occasions. The first was as a team-mate of Gaetano's, the second with Andrea as coach of the Italian national team. I'll never forget those experiences. In the first instance I was full of awe; in the second, admiration. The lesson was pretty clear: people who keep their voices down reap the rewards later on. And those rewards include the unconditional respect of the people round about them.

In this book Andrea says, and I quote: "After the 2014 World Cup in Brazil, I'm going to retire from international football. I'll be hanging up my heart. Until that day, nobody must dare ask me to stop, apart from Cesare Prandelli, should he have tactical reasons."

I can say for definite that I won't. The most difficult thing for a coach is to say "enough" to a real talent. A choice like that ideally should be made in tandem with the player. But, really, it's not even worth discussing: I can't think of a single reason why I'd leave Andrea out between now and the World Cup.

People like him and Gigi Buffon embody the true spirit of Italy. If everyone had the same respect for that shirt, our world would be a better place. After so many battles, their motivation remains exactly the same as it was the first day they stepped into the environment.

Andrea was born dreaming, and to allow us to dream. Thinking about it, he's still the kid I saw all those years ago, pulling on a Brescia strip that was somewhat bigger than him. There was a time when Atalanta Youths could have signed him, but it would have been a real insult to Brescia. We actually called a meeting to discuss the possibility of bringing him in, but our president Percassi, an enlightened man, understood that we'd have caused a diplomatic incident.

I'll never forget his words: "Pirlo stays where he is. People like him should be left in peace. He needs to keep enjoying himself and playing with happiness. I don't want him to feel any kind of pressure. He must remain a player who belongs to everyone."

Percassi had understood perfectly. Percassi had understood Pirlo.

---

1   Literally: "the pupils"

2   Literally: "the very young ones"

3   Having started out with Atalanta, Scirea, a sweeper, was at the heart of Juventus and Italy success in the late 1970s and 1980s, including the 1982 World Cup

Chapter 1

A pen. Beautiful, granted, but still just a pen. A Cartier: shiny, a little bit heavier than a biro and emblazoned with the Milan club crest. But still just a pen.

The ink cartridge was blue. Plain old blue. I looked at the pen, spun it round in my hand like an infant examining its first soft toy. I studied the thing from a few different angles, seeking out hidden depths and meanings. Trying to understand. Trying so hard that I felt a headache coming on and a few drops of sweat slide down my face.

Finally, the flash of inspiration arrived. Mystery solved: it was, indeed, just a pen. No added extras. Its inventor had left it at that. Deliberately? Who knows.

Suddenly I heard a voice. "For goodness' sake, don't use it to sign for Juventus."

Adriano Galliani had at least managed to come up with a decent line. As a leaving present, I'd have expected something a little more than his perfect comic timing. Ten years at Milan, finished, just like that. Still, I raised a smile, because I know how to laugh, loud and long.

"Thanks for everything, Andrea."

As the club vice president and chief executive spoke, sat safely behind his desk, I had a look around. I knew his office like the back of my hand. It was a vault in the heart of Milan's old administrative base on the Via Turati. I had happy memories of that room: other contracts, other pens. And yet I'd never noticed some of the photos on the walls, or had only done so distractedly. Those photos had a weighty history, but the prestige was subtly understated.

There was every type of photo on display. Memories of glory days and once-in-a-lifetime occasions. Trophies lifted into the air; clouds always being pushed just that little bit out of shot. My picture was being taken down from the frame, but not by force. Getting bored of Milan was a risk I didn't want to run. That's why at that last meeting I was sorry, but just the right amount. Galliani and Tullio Tinti, my agent, both felt the same way.

We said our goodbyes without regret. In the space of half an hour (probably not even that), I was out of there. When you're in love, it's time you need. When the feeling's gone, having an excuse can help.

"Andrea, our coach Massimiliano Allegri reckons that if you stay, you won't be able to play in front of the defence. He's got a different role in mind for you. Still in midfield, but on the left."

One small detail: I still thought I could give of my best playing in front of the defence. If the sea's deep, a fish can breathe. If you put him just under the surface, he'll get by, but it's not quite the same thing.

"Even with you sitting on the bench or in the stand we've won the league. And you know, Andrea, the strategy's changed this year. If you're over 30, we're only offering a year's extension."

Another small detail: I've never felt old, not even at that very moment. Only indirectly did I get the impression that people were trying to make out I was finished. Even now, I struggle to get my head round their reasoning.

"Thanks, but I really can't accept. There's a three-year deal on the table at Juventus."

It was a polite 'no' for Milan, without money even entering the conversation that spring afternoon in 2011. Not once in those 30 minutes was it ever mentioned. I wanted to be thought of as important, a key player in the club's plans, not someone about to be thrown on the scrapheap.

It was, it seemed, the end of an era and I felt in need of something new. Alarm bells had been ringing ever since the middle of what turned out to be my last season at the club, one ruined by a couple of injuries. I arrived at Milanello for training and realised that I didn't want to go into the dressing room. Didn't want to get changed, didn't want to work.

I got on well with everyone and had a normal kind of relationship with Allegri – there was just something in the air. I recognised the walls that over the years had sheltered and protected me, but now I was starting to see cracks. I could sense some kind of draught that was out to make me sick.

That inner urge to go somewhere else, to breathe a different air, became ever more pressing and intense. The poetry that had always surrounded me was now becoming routine. It wasn't something I could ignore. Even the fans maybe wanted a bit of relief. For so many years they'd applauded me at San Siro of a Sunday (and a Saturday, a Tuesday, a Wednesday...), but now perhaps they wanted to stick new faces in their Panini album, hear new stories being told. They'd got used to the things I did, my movements, my creations. They weren't awestruck any more. In their eyes, the extraordinary was in real danger of becoming normal.

You can't be Pirlo any more. That was a difficult idea to accept. In actual fact, it was deeply unjust. It brought on the start of a sore stomach as I searched in vain for that lost stimulus.

I sat down with Alessandro Nesta: friend, brother, team-mate, roomie. A man with whom I'd shared a thousand adventures, and about as many snacks. At half-time in one of our never-ending football games on the PlayStation, I confessed all. "Sandro, I'm leaving."

He didn't seem surprised. "I'm really sorry to hear that. But it's the right decision."

After my family, he was the first to find out. I kept him up to speed with everything: step by step, tear by tear. Some weeks were harder than others. A countdown was underway inside of me, but it's never easy to have to leave a place you know everything about. Including all its secrets.

Milan is a little world apart. One that gave much more than it took and, without a shadow of a doubt, stirred strong feelings in me. Sometimes it was dejection mixed with sadness, other times raw emotion. At any rate, it taught me a valuable life lesson: it's good to cry. Tears are a visible demonstration of who you are; an undeniable truth. I didn't hold back. I cried and wasn't ashamed to do so.

My boarding card wasn't so much in my hand as in my head. I was like a passenger at the airport a second before they turn round and wave goodbye to family, friends and enemies. Whether it's a little or a lot, you always leave something behind.

I phoned my agent every day, especially in the period when I was supposed to be recovering from injury, but the desire to really throw myself into it just wasn't there. Or at least it wasn't the same as it had been at one time. Massimo Ambrosini and then Mark van Bommel were playing in front of the defence. My house had been broken into – by friends, and not out of badness, but ransacked all the same. I'd been evicted from my much-loved garden, with its patchy grass and bald spots.

"Tullio – any news?"

There always was; and it was always good to excellent. The more ill at ease I felt at Milan, the greater the pull I seemed to exert in the marketplace – a strange rule of football. I was like the X on a treasure trail. Everyone made enquiries, even Inter. Talk about earthquakes in Milan: if that one had come off, it would probably have broken the seismograph.

They rang up Tinti and asked a simple question. "Would Andrea come back here?" Tinti said he'd put it to me. We decided we wouldn't rule anything out straight away. "Let's hear what they want," I said.

Turns out they wanted me. But they were slow. Impressive, certainly, but slow. Before they could get down to serious negotiations, they had to wait and see how the season ended up, who was going to be their coach in the new campaign and what the club's plans and objectives were going to look like. I was contacted directly just the once. I remember it well: it was a Monday morning and the season had just finished.

"Hi Andrea, it's Leo."

On the line was Leonardo, at that point still Inter coach.

"*Ciao* Leo."

"Listen, everything's finally sorted. I've had the green light from president Moratti. We can begin to talk."

He told me some great things about Inter; said he felt really energised and in his element there. It could have been a nice challenge – going back to somewhere I'd already been. Returning to the other side after 10 straight years at Milan, nine of them extraordinary. Leonardo could have helped me settle back in, had he not headed off to Paris St Germain and their sheiks a few weeks down the line.

"Andrea, in the new Inter, you'll have a key role."

I did think about it, but I wouldn't have been capable of actually doing it. It would have been too much; an affront that the Milan fans wouldn't have deserved.

"Thanks Leo, but I can't. Last night I signed for Juventus."

I'll never say which pen I used.

Chapter 2

Discarded. Tossed aside. Thrown on the scrapheap. Or maybe deleted, demolished, defused. Or perhaps even filed away, abandoned, buried. Chucked out.

If certain people at Milan really did want me to end up like that, their plans ran aground. A Titanic in miniature, if you like, with the famous Milanese fog playing the role of the icebergs.

I actually want to thank the people who got their sums so badly wrong. If the calculator hadn't gone a bit crazy, had the crystal ball that predicts the future not been handled by their overly rough hands, I would never have got to feel like just another guy. A normal person. A six-out-of-10 kind of player.

For a brief period, I was living in a kind of virtual reality. I was the other Andrea Pirlo, the one those people wanted to make out I was. The Pirlo I could have been but instead never became. They treated me like I was nothing special, making me wait with bated breath. In reality, it had the opposite effect, strengthening people's conviction that I was something more.

As a kid, and then as an adolescent, I tried to rail against a concept conveyed through a few different words: "unique", "special", "preordained". Over time, I learned to live with it and use it to my advantage.

It wasn't easy for me or for the people who care about me. From an early age, I knew I was a better player than the others, and for that very reason tongues were soon wagging. Everyone talked about me; too much in fact, and not always in a good way. On more than one occasion, my dad, Luigi, had to leave the stand where he was watching and flee to the other side of the pitch, to avoid hearing the nasty comments made by other parents.

He got out of there to avoid reacting, or perhaps to avoid becoming too sad. He had nothing to be ashamed of, and so he ignored them, striding away ever faster, like an Italian Forrest Gump. He'd only stop when he reached a quieter spot that was safer and more sheltered.

Unfortunately not even my mum, Lidia, was spared the angry outbursts.

"Who does that kid think he is? Maradona?"

That's the line they used most often. Spurred on by their jealousy, they'd say it deliberately loudly, trying to provoke a reaction. They didn't seem to realise they were actually paying me the biggest compliment. Maradona, for fuck's sake! It's like calling a gymnast Jury Chechi, a basketball player Michael Jordan, or a top model Naomi Campbell. It's like calling Silvio Berlusconi a giant.

By definition it was an unfair fight: adults picking on a little kid. Just plain wrong. The only way I could defend myself was by doing things that would amaze. Precisely what they were accusing me of in the first place.

I bore the mark of a non-existent sin, but was protected by an invisible suit of armour. One that every so often couldn't prevent the odd lunging knife or poisoned arrow slipping through. A whole bunch of them hit me one afternoon when I was 14 and playing for the Brescia youths. I say playing for them, but in actual fact they were playing against me.

"Pass me the ball."

Silence.

Strange: I'd shouted it loudly, and my Italian was pretty good.

"Guys, pass me the ball."

Still nothing. A silence so deafening that I could hear my words echoing around.

"Is something going on here?"

Silence again. Everyone making out they were deaf.

Nobody would pass me the ball. My team-mates were playing amongst themselves, leaving me out completely. I was there but they couldn't see me. Or better, they *could* see me, but chose to pretend I wasn't there. They were treating me like some kind of leper, just because I was better than them at football.

I flitted about like a ghost, dying on the inside. There was a mutiny taking place against me. They wouldn't even talk to me, wouldn't even look in my direction. Absolutely nothing.

"Are you going to give me the ball or not?"

Silence.

I blew up and burst out crying. Right there on the pitch, in front of 21 opponents. Eleven on the other team, and 10 supposedly on mine. Once I started I just couldn't stop. I ran and cried. I sprinted and cried. I stood still and cried. I was completely dejected and depressed. Most of all, I was an adolescent. And that sort of thing shouldn't happen to someone so young. At that age, you should be scoring goals and celebrating. But the fact that I scored so many upset a lot of people.

It was in that precise moment that my career, still in its formative stages, took a turn down the right path. I had a choice: get pissed off and stop, or get pissed off and keep playing. Playing *my* way. The second option struck me as more intelligent, and something I could work on straight away.

Off I went and gathered the ball. Once, twice, a hundred times. Me against the rest of the world. I was like some kind of noble crusader. Nobody wanted to play with me? Fine then; I'd be my own team. It wasn't like I didn't have the weaponry. Ten of them would struggle to score, but I'd manage it all on my own. I'd dribble past every last one of them, including the kids wearing the same colour of shirt as me.

They'd all got it so wrong: I didn't have the slightest intention of behaving like a superstar. The truth is a lot simpler: that's just how I was made. I was acting on pure instinct, not riding a flight of fancy. I'd spy a pass, the chance to bring out a trick or an opportunity to score and it was already done. I'd outpace even myself, especially when it came to thinking.

Even in those early days I was someone who always had to deliver; always had to maintain high standards. For everyone else, it was okay to have an average game. If I did, it was a failure.

Right from the start, they said I always seemed tired, as if I couldn't go on. Truth is they were taken in by the way I moved around the pitch. I looked like I was idling, always taking small steps. Small steps for me, giant leaps for mankind. Or something like that.

Venting my emotions out on the pitch all those years ago was like releasing a coiled spring. If there are too many people around, I'll tend not to speak all that much. I'll get worked up, for good or bad, without letting on. But that afternoon it was a different story.

I conducted a long and silent discussion with my inner self. Looking back, it bordered on madness:

Andrea, a gift like yours shouldn't be a millstone. It's true, you're better than the others, and you should be proud of that fact. Mother Nature was kind to you; she was on good form the day you were born. She gave you the magic touch – now go take advantage of it.

You want to be a footballer? That's the dream that's attached itself to you? The others want to be astronauts but you couldn't give a fuck about going into space? Well then, go and pick up that ball. Give it a stroke: it belongs to you. The jealous folks don't deserve it. They're trying to steal that special part of you. Smile. Be happy. Make this moment brilliant and then make many more just like it.

Go on, take that leap and if you can, take your father with you. The people giving chase will soon fall behind. It's written in the stars. Go, Andrea. GO!

Even today, I'm not completely convinced I'm unique or irreplaceable. But I struggle to explain that to people who are used to making superficial judgments about me. I have reached one conclusion, though. I think I've understood that there *is* a secret: I perceive the game in a different way. It's a question of viewpoints, of having a wide field of vision. Being able to see the bigger picture.

Your classic midfielder looks downfield and sees the forwards. I'll focus instead on the space between me and them where I can work the ball through. It's more a question of geometry than tactics. The space seems bigger to me. It looks easier to get in behind – a wall that can easily be knocked down.

People have compared me to Gianni Rivera[4], saying that side of my game reminds them of him. I've never seen him play, not even on video, so I can't say whether they're right or wrong. I've never looked at another player, past or present, and thought they were similar to me. I suppose there's always time, but I'm not on the lookout for clones; it's not something that interests me. After all, Dolly won't ever be the same as the other sheep.

I don't feel pressure, either. I don't give a toss about it. I spent the afternoon of Sunday, July 9, 2006, in Berlin sleeping and playing the PlayStation. In the evening, I went out and won the World Cup.

From a mental point of view, my not entirely inadvertent tutor was Mircea Lucescu, the coach who plucked me from the Brescia youths aged 15 and put me straight into the big boys' world of the first team. I found myself training with 30-somethings who were a little bit put out at me getting under their feet. They were twice as old as me and, some days, twice as nasty.

"Andrea, keep playing like you did in the youth team."

That was the first phrase Lucescu whispered to me and, like a good little soldier, I obeyed. Not everyone took it well, especially the senior players in the dressing room. They were among the most listened to and respected out on the pitch, and were like old men compared to me.

One day I took the ball past one of them three times in a row. The fourth time was fatal. He committed the worst foul of all time, carrying out a premeditated assault on my ankle. There was no point trying to make out he hadn't meant it – nobody would have believed him.

He, too, thought I was acting like a superstar when, in reality, all I was doing was following Lucescu's instruction. The coach gave me a wink and said: "Don't worry, everything's fine. And make sure to try that again, please."

He spoke to me with kindness then turned to the rest of the team and said: "Give the ball to Pirlo; he knows how to look after it."

It's the story of a strange friendship, between a person and an object. I knew how to do certain things with a football without even having tried them. My first real triumph was when my team-mates kicked me less often than they passed to me. On my first day of training, the ratio was 10:1 (ten attempted murders to one pass reaching me, almost always by mistake). Over time things improved, eventually reaching a point where there were consistently more passes than fouls.

That made me happy, especially for my dad, who could then get a season ticket in the best leather seats right in the middle of the stand. He didn't need to bring along his earplugs any more. The jealous folks were right where we'd left them, back at the youth team pitches.

---

4   Rivera is a Milan and Italy legend. A stylish playmaker, he won three Serie A
    titles and two European Cups, as well as the 1968 European Championship

Chapter 3

They weren't bad kids, the ones I played with in the Brescia youths. But they did have a very serious problem; one that always got the better of them. They were running scared of their own dreams. Dreams that weighed them down and eventually crushed them.

They thought of me as the Bogey Man; someone trying to kill their future. I held out my hand to drag them up, but instead they turned their back on me. They fell behind then pulled out of the race to become professional players.

For me, it's always better to keep chasing down the guy in front and maybe finish second, rather than stopping altogether. It's a shame they never understood that.

I know fine well what was going through their minds when they found themselves in quicksand, corroded and imprisoned by the worm of jealousy. I can almost hear them even now: a chorus of voices all screaming the wish that was dying in front of their eyes: "We want to play for Barcelona or Real Madrid!"

I know because they told me. I know because I told

them. Becoming a footballer is only the first half of the silent prayer a kid offers up to the sky or confides to his teacher in a primary school essay. The second part is the name of the team he wants to play for.

Spain was right at the top of our list, an undisputed king that had us utterly captivated. It was a flight of fancy, an ambitious project put together word by word while we had our playtime snack. We wanted to turn our fruit juice into sangria, or perhaps even *cerveza*.

Twice I almost managed the miracle.

It's the summer of 2006, we've just won the World Cup, and I'm thoroughly drunk on life. I go out and about on my bike in the quiet little streets of Forte dei Marmi[5] and, as I pass by on the seafront, people stop and pat me on the back. Fans say hello and I do likewise; there's a nod of recognition for each and every one of them.

"Hello, Andrea."

"*Buenos dias.*"

"What a lovely afternoon, Andrea."

"*Buenas tardes.*"

"Sweet dreams, Andrea."

"*Buenas noches.*"

"Ciao, Andrea."

"*Hola.*"

"We're heading back to Milan; see you soon, Andrea."

"*Adios.*"

"Coming to the usual place in a little while for a drink, Andrea?"

"*Hasta ahora.*"

They must have thought that beating France in the final

had fried my brain, but there was something they didn't know. They were missing a vital piece of the story, namely that as things stood, I belonged to Real Madrid, not Milan. I was a Madrid player in my head, my heart and my soul. I had a five-year contract sitting waiting, and a salary that was out of this world.

It seemed that certain people at Milan had got themselves into one too many scrapes – or at least that was the story doing the rounds. *Calciopoli* [6] was the second most popular topic of conversation back then, a close second to Italy's penalty shootout triumph in Germany. One day you'd read that we were going to be relegated to Serie B, the next that we were looking at a 15-point penalty. The next again day they'd be talking about us handing back trophies and having our titles removed from the record books. After a while I began to suspect that it wasn't Mark David Chapman who killed John Lennon. It had been one of the Milan directors.

The whole thing was an absolute shambles. Nobody, least of all me, had a clue what was going on and what Milan's fate would actually be. One thing I was sure of, though: I would never drop down to Serie B. And if I had to leave, I wouldn't feel like a traitor. You always want to be ambitious and play for a noble cause. There was no way I was going to pay for other people's sins, if that's what they turned out to be. I've always believed that those who make the mess are responsible for cleaning it up. If you break something, you pay.

The Madrid coach Fabio Capello phoned. And then Franco Baldini, their director of football. Everyone wanted to speak to me. I had a word with my agent and asked him to find out what Milan were saying about it all.

Shortly after, I was due back at Milanello. To make the Champions League proper, we had to get through a qualifier against Red Star Belgrade. I was trying to reach the very top of the skyscraper and here we were on the ground floor. Those of us who had been at the World Cup were in line for only 10 days' holiday before training started again, but it was at that point Tullio said to me: "Hold off on going back. Let me speak to Real. If you really want a change of scene from Forte dei Marmi, head back to your house in Brescia. And keep your mobile on – in a little while you'll get a call."

No sooner had he said it than the phone started ringing. Nostradamus was a mere amateur compared to our Tullio.

"Hello Andrea, it's Fabio Capello here." Only one of the most successful coaches in the history of the sport.

"Hello, coach. How are you?"

"I'm great, and I imagine you're even better. Come and join us. We've just signed Emerson from Juventus and you're the man to play beside him in midfield."

"Okay then."

He didn't need much time to convince me. Less than a minute, I reckon. Not least because I'd already seen the contract. My agent had studied it in great detail and then shot off to Madrid. We were like two young lovers, Tullio and I. Teenagers with each other on speed dial. The phone lines were red hot.

"Andrea, we're on."

"I'm really happy about that, Tullio."

I pictured myself in that white jersey. Pristine, and at the same time aggressive; a mean streak running through its unusual purity. My thoughts often wandered to the Santiago Bernabeu, the temple, a ground that struck terror into opponents. Bruised and battered slaves at the king's banquet.

"What do we do now then, Tullio?"

"Let's go for lunch in a few days."

"Where? Meson Txistu in Plaza de Angel Carbajo?"

"No, Andrea; not Madrid. Milanello."

"What do you mean 'Milanello'? Are you stupid?"

"Nope, you heard right: Milanello. We haven't got Galliani's approval yet."

Ah yes, the pen guy.

The menu was always the same: I knew it off by heart. Antipasto, starter, main course and then the legendary ice cream with crunchy bits on top.

We met in the room used for team meals, halfway between the kitchens and the hall with the hearth where Berlusconi would pound away on the piano and tell various kinds of jokes. Equidistant between the most modest part of the complex and the richest. Between a symbol of humility and one of unabashed power. Between a place where people sweat buckets earning relatively little, and a spot where they earn a fortune sweating just the right amount.

I, meanwhile, was floating between Milan and Real Madrid.

Tullio spoke first. "Andrea's going to sign for Real."

Then me: "Yes..."

Then it was Galliani, staring straight at me. "Andrea, my friend, you're not going anywhere."

He pulled out a little case from under the table. That made me smile, thinking it had been just as well hidden as Monica Lewinsky under Bill Clinton's desk in the Oval Office (every now and then I'm carried away by these crazy trains of thought).

A contract then appeared from the case, with Mr Biro adding, "You're not leaving, because you're going to sign this. It's for five years, and we've left the salary details blank so you can write in whatever you like."

Tullio just about ripped it out of my hands. "I'll keep hold of this."

He took his time, brought it home, read it and read it again. I went off to the national team training camp at Coverciano[7] and, for a few days, I didn't hear anything. I thought it was a done deal: I was thinking in Spanish, dreaming in Spanish. My imagination was in overdrive, flying off to Madrid and landing somewhere between Plaza Mayor and Puerta del Sol.

And then my agent phoned me.

"Sign for Milan. Right now, they'll not let you leave."

"No…"

"Yes."

"Ok, fine."

People maybe think decisions like that take an eternity – hours, days, or even months, sapping your physical and mental energy. It's almost never the case, because often your instincts will be telling you one thing but a clause in your contract obliges you to do something else entirely. In that sort of scenario, it doesn't take long to say 'no', even if you're doing so reluctantly.

You're then forced to tell the media a lot of crap; provided, of course, that they manage to ask you the right question. If they enquire whether it's right you'd practically signed for Madrid, you're duty-bound to respond hiding behind well-worn clichés and half-truths. You read a dull, lifeless script written by press officers with no talent or creative spark.

"No, that's not the case. I'm perfectly happy at Milan."

Fuck off!

It's a pity it went the way it did. I'd have signed for Real in a heartbeat. They're a club with more glamour than Milan; more prospects, more appeal, more everything. They strike fear in their opponents, whoever they happen to be.

All that said, I had the consolation of winning the Champions League at the end of the season. It could have gone a lot worse.

Capello and his assistant Franco Baldini weren't exactly happy when Tullio told them I wouldn't be emigrating. The idea has always stuck with Baldini, however. Every time I see him, he comes over, smiles and launches into the same story. "I've never managed to bring you to a club where I've been working. Sooner or later, though…"

He tried to take me to Roma before I signed for Juventus. I just wasn't sure of the situation and the circumstances, even though I trusted him. He's great at his job; he's got style. The new ownership structure was what concerned me – I just wasn't convinced by it. "We're going to build a great Roma," Baldini kept insisting, but he couldn't tell me much, if anything, about the Americans who had bought a majority stake.

I got suspicious. If the "new" club had been up and running, had it been a reality and not just words, perhaps I would have signed. Rome is a beautiful city. The people are special and the climate's fantastic. But the fact is that at that point, nobody had even seen the future president, Thomas DiBenedetto. And the hypothetical trio of new directors, Pallotta-D'Amore-Ruane, sounded like something from the credits for a song at the San Remo Music Festival. "Composed by Pallotta-D'Amore-Ruane, conducted by Vince Tempera[8]."

Surrounded by the flowers of the Ariston Theatre, the MC could easily have introduced that night's singer with those words. The name of the song? Thanks anyway, Roma[9].

And thanks also to Spain. *Siempre.* Because as well as Real Madrid, I was courted by Barcelona, the other half of the dream.

5   A seaside resort in northern Tuscany, popular with tourists

6   A match-rigging scandal that saw Juventus relegated to Serie B and stripped of the 2005 and 2006 Serie A titles. Milan, Lazio, Fiorentina and Reggina also received points penalties

7   Located on the outskirts of Florence

8   A prominent figure in Italian music, Tempera is known for his output as a producer, arranger, conductor and performer

9   *Grazie Roma* by Antonello Venditti was a big hit in the wake of the club's 1983 *scudetto* win and is still sung by fans today

Chapter 4

After the wheel, the PlayStation is the best invention of all time. And ever since it's existed, I've been Barcelona, apart from a brief spell way back at the start when I'd go Milan.

I can't say with any certainty how many virtual matches I've played over the last few years but, roughly speaking, it must be at least four times the number of real ones.

Pirlo v Nesta was a classic duel back in our Milanello days. We'd get in early, have breakfast at 9am and then shut ourselves in our room and hit the PlayStation until 11. Training would follow, then we'd be back on the computer games until four in the afternoon. Truly a life of sacrifice.

Our head-to-heads were pure adrenaline. I'd go Barcelona and so would Sandro. Barca v Barca. The first player I'd pick was the quickest one, Samuel Eto'o, but I'd still end up losing a lot of the time. I'd get pissed off and hurl away my controller before asking Sandro for a rematch. And then I'd lose again.

It's not like I could use the excuse that his coach was better than mine: it was Pep Guardiola for him and Pep

Guardiola for me. At least in terms of our manager we set out on a level footing.

One day we thought about kidnapping him. The flesh and bones, real-life version that is. It was August 25, 2010, and we were with Milan at the Nou Camp for the Gamper pre-season tournament. We thought better of our hostage-taking in the end. To avoid constantly falling out, we'd have needed to saw him in two when we got back to Italy, and that wouldn't have been a good idea. How the poor thing would have suffered.

As it transpired, the notion of abduction had crossed Guardiola's mind before ours. That very night at the Nou Camp, he whisked me away from my nearest and dearest. Looking back, perhaps those people weren't actually as close to me as I thought but, anyway, on with the story.

At the end of the game, everyone was on the trail of Zlatan Ibrahimovic, a ticking timebomb of a madman who had been wound up by his agent (the legendary Mino Raiola). The Swede was set on a collision course with Barcelona and on the verge of signing for Milan. A few of my team-mates sought him out to try to encourage him to make the switch, while some of his friends from Barcelona were also on his case, armed with the opposite recommendation. And then there were the journalists, looking to force a few words from him, which didn't exactly take them long.

"I'd love to play at San Siro in the same team as Ronaldinho," he said. "The coach here doesn't even talk to me. In the last six months, he's spoken to me twice."

There was no mystery in that – Guardiola was saving his words for me. Taking advantage of the spotlight being momentarily trained not on him but Ibrahimovic, he invited me into his office.

As I came out of the dressing room, I'd noticed one of his childhood friends and trusted lieutenants waiting there for me. His task that night had turned him into a flip-flop wearing secret agent, but Manel Estiarte in a previous life had been the best water polo player of all time. Only the second man in history capable of walking on water.

"Andrea, come with me. The coach wants to meet you."

I struggled to recognise him without his swimming cap. But then I looked at him again and got a whiff of chlorine.

"Okay then, *vamos*."

I didn't need to be asked twice. In I went. The room was furnished in sober fashion, and there was some red wine on the table. "Always a good start," I muttered to myself. Thankfully the most envied coach in the word didn't hear me. His way of speaking is very similar to mine – not really tenor style, let's say.

"Make yourself comfortable, Andrea," he began, his Italian absolutely perfect.

I wasn't really bothered about much else in that room besides the person who had summoned me. Guardiola was sitting in an armchair. He began to tell me about Barcelona, saying that it's a world apart, a perfect machine that pretty much invented itself. He wore a white shirt and a pair of dark trousers whose colour matched that of his tie. He was elegant in the extreme, much like his conversation.

"Thank you for agreeing to meet me."

"Thank you for inviting me."

"We need you here, Andrea."

You could tell he wasn't a man to beat about the bush. After a couple of minutes, he'd cut straight to the chase. As a player, his job had been to conduct the play and as a manager he'd learned to attack, always with impeccable style.

"We're already very strong, I really couldn't ask for better, but you'd be the icing on the cake. We're looking for a midfielder to alternate with Xavi, Iniesta and Busquets, and that midfielder is you. You've got all the attributes to play for Barcelona, and one in particular – you're world class."

During that half hour I largely kept quiet and let him speak. I listened and, at most, nodded my head. I was so taken aback by the summons that my reflexes had slowed. I was more dazed than excited: shaken by the situation, but in a really positive way.

"You know what, Andrea: we've made this approach because that's how we do things round here. We don't waste time. We want to buy you right now, and we've already spoken to Milan. They've said 'no', but we'll not give up: we're Barcelona. We're used to hearing certain answers but, in the end, things pretty much always change. We'll try again with Milan. In the meantime, start making a few moves with them as well."

Nobody had said a thing to me until then. Without even knowing, I was the object of some remarkable negotiations in the football luxury goods market.

"If you come here, you'll find yourself in a unique place. La Masia, our youth academy, is our pride and joy – there's nothing like it at any other club. It runs like clockwork; it's a philharmonic orchestra where bum notes aren't permitted. Every year, players arrive from there ready to wear our shirt.

"Our champions are home-made; apart from you, that is. What we do is all very wonderful, but all very demanding, too. Sometimes winning can be draining."

I would never have expected it. Perhaps I'd spent so much time on the PlayStation that I'd ended up inside it, sucked into a parallel universe by my favourite hobby and now at the mercy of a puppeteer with some kind of enchanted hand.

"You've got to come here, Andrea. I've always liked you as a player. I want to coach you."

I immediately thought of Sandro – he'd die of jealousy when I told him. I was taking away the 50% of Guardiola that belonged to him.

"Even though Milan have said 'no' for the moment, we're not giving up. Let's see what happens."

As with Real Madrid (in fact, even more so than with Real Madrid), I'd have crawled to Barcelona on all fours. At that time, they were the best team in the world – what more needs to be said? Their brand of football hadn't been seen in a long time; all little first-time passes and an almost insane ability to maintain possession.

Theirs was a basic philosophy – "the ball's ours, and we're going to keep it" – mixed with intuitive understanding and movement so impressive that it seemed orchestrated by God himself. A Rolex with Swatch batteries. Utterly refined, extremely long lasting.

"Let's talk again soon," said Guardiola. "Have a safe journey back to Milan and let's hope you're not there for long."

"Thanks again. It's been a very interesting chat."

I left his office in a daze. I was just about last onto the Milan team bus, but nobody took any notice. With their noses pressed up against the windows, lots of players were peering at the scene unfolding outside. Both curious and impressed, they watched Ibrahimovic walking his tightrope.

At one end, Barcelona, and a fire that was dying out. At the other, Milan, and a spark turning into a flame.

We were heading in different directions, Ibrahimovic and I. The world knew all about his situation, but nothing about mine. If these initial advances became a full-blown love affair, I'd wind up part of a truly great club and be thrown into a new challenge. I'd have liked that, a lot.

The discussions went on for a while and, ultimately, Milan didn't give in. I suppose it was always going to go like that. Back then, they still thought I had all my faculties and so they kept me, without ever getting involved in full-on negotiations. There were words, brief chats, a little bit of back and forth, but nothing more substantial.

I'd have considered myself fortunate to be coached by Guardiola, because he really puts his stamp on teams. He builds them, moulds them, guides them, berates them, nurtures them. He makes them great. He takes them to a higher level; a place beyond mere football. Ibrahimovic thought he was insulting him when he called him 'The Philosopher', but when you think about it, that's actually a nice compliment.

Being a philosopher is to think, seek wisdom and have principles that guide and influence what you do. It's to give meaning to things, find your way in the world, believe that in the end, in every instance, good will overcome evil even if there's a bit of suffering along the way.

Guardiola has taken all that and applied it to football, an imperfect science. He racked his brains and dispersed the fog, more through hard work than mere thought. What he's achieved hasn't been about miracles, rather a gentle programming of his players. His style is *crèma catalana* –

easily digestible. It's virtual reality mixed with real life; a swim between the shores of fantasy and reality with Estiarte by his side.

In other words, we're talking PlayStation.

Chapter 5

Guardiola lives in a Zen-like corner of the PlayStation, an unused portion of the hard drive. It's a secret room where shadows dance and on July 9, 2006, the day of the World Cup final, I camped out there as well.

It's a strange place – only a few people end up there, and even then only by chance. Mine was a rapid but unforgettable incursion, one that's more difficult to understand than to recount.

The situation completely possesses you. You feel like a prisoner, but also totally at ease. One minute you're suffocating and the next you're breathing in mountain air. You close your eyes and see a whole load of things, then you open them and the colours of the painting dissolve around you, re-emerging in different forms. The image loses its outline and your mind flies away, a hot air balloon swollen by a thousand thoughts, each of them dangerously heavy.

I've got a fair few kilometres under my belt, but it's the short distances that wear me out. They're tests of your mental stamina rather than your speed. For Neil Armstrong, it was walking on the surface of the moon and, in my case, the ultra-green pitch of the Olympiastadion[10].

Thinking about that World Cup final against France, there's a moment that feels very much my own. When Marcello Lippi, the Italy coach, came up to me at the end of normal time, bells started to toll in my head. I'd actually have preferred the volume to be a bit louder, but the noise wasn't sufficient to prevent the two words that great coach uttered from reaching my ears unhindered.

"You're first."

We both knew what he meant by that: first to take a penalty. Being first on the spot, kicking off that torture in the biggest, most incredible game that a player can play or imagine… that's not necessarily good news. It means they think you're the best, but it also means that if you miss, you're first on the list of dickheads.

I'll go right; no left, because that's the keeper's weaker side. No, I'll put it in the top corner, there's no way he's reaching that. But what if I get it wrong and the ball flies off into the stand?

My thoughts were all over the place, drunken ideas at the wheel of fairground dodgems. I really didn't know what to do, but the worst was still to come. When a match is decided in that way, one man against millions with the keeper trying to save a nation, there's a sadistic group ritual that leads you to your fate. It's a sacrificial procession that beckons you to jump on board.

The two teams gather in the centre circle and the next player up has to make his way from there to the penalty spot. It's an experience I wouldn't wish on anyone. It's barely 50 metres, but it's a truly terrible journey, right through the heart of your fear. The comparison with the dead man walking, pulling himself along the green mile is exaggerated and not the most appropriate, but it does get across the idea.

I got up to head to the spot. It was my turn and I acted on instinct.

I'll hit it straight down the middle, put a bit of height on it. Barthez will definitely dive and there's no way he's getting to it, even with his feet.

That moment really is a torment. A blizzard of agony. There's a storm raging inside and all around you. The journey from centre circle to penalty spot was crammed with violent emotions. I opted to walk slowly. On some kind of subconscious level, I didn't want to miss anything. I wanted to take absolutely everything from the moment. I vowed never to forget that little outing that went beyond everything and turned seconds into hours and each step into a dramatic tale.

I didn't really succeed. A good few things passed me by, and all that's left in my mind are a few isolated clips. I stared at the pitch, as if it wasn't exactly the same as every other one I'd played on, as if my studs were gripping onto something softer than the usual clumps of turf. I'd had my children's names printed on my boots and perhaps that's the reason I was trying to move with the utmost care, to avoid doing them any harm.

Every so often, I'd lift my head to stare at an indeterminate spot on the horizon, right at the end of the journey. Instead of seeing Barthez, I'd get distracted by the photographers' flashbulbs as they huddled behind the goals.

Let's hope they don't blind me. Fingers crossed they don't annoy me too much.

I was in the penalty box holding my breath. I picked up

the ball. It was as heavy as the pressure bearing down on me from all sides. I tried to catch Buffon's eye; I could have done with a nod, a gesture, a little bit of advice, anything. But Gigi had enough problems of his own to worry about and didn't have time for mine.

Caressing the ball was something I had to do. I then lifted my eyes to the heavens and asked for help because if God exists, there's no way he's French. I took a long, intense breath. That breath was mine, but it could have been the manual worker who struggles to make it to the end of the month, the rich businessman who's a bit of a shit, the teacher, the student, the Italian expats who never left our side during the tournament, the well-to-do Milanese *signora*, the hooker on the street corner. In that moment, I was all of them.

You won't believe me, but it was right in that very moment I understood what a great thing it is to be Italian. It's a truly priceless privilege. I never got the same understanding from the empty speeches of the politicians. They don't know what they're talking about as they grab and stick their snouts in the trough. Nor did I experience the same emotion in the history books I've studied – perhaps because all too often I kept them closed and allowed the dust to build up. My parents were right when they said that was a big mistake.

Never would I have thought that the instant before taking a penalty could open my mind so marvellously and give me this higher understanding. I saw the inner workings of a motor car that was imperfect, full of defects, badly driven, old and worn, and yet still utterly unique. Italy's a country you love precisely because it's like that.

My penalty went in. Even if I'd missed, the lesson would have remained. Perhaps it would actually have been amplified by the resulting desperation. It's incredible to know that what you're feeling is shared by millions of people in the same way, at the same time, for the same reasons, in cities that moments before were rivals or at least too dissimilar to find any sort of common ground. That lukewarm shiver a second before I stuck the ball in the net is the most vivid sensation I've ever felt.

We'd talk about those moments in the months afterwards. I soon discovered I wasn't the only one who had come back from Germany with lofty topics of conversation.

That penalty also helps define me. As usual, nobody will believe me but, in my own mind, I'm much more the Pirlo who stuck the ball down the middle at World Cup 2006 than the Pirlo of the inspired chip against England in the quarter-finals of Euro 2012. Even if the motivation was the same in both cases: selecting the best option to minimise the risk of error.

To be clear, I didn't do a Francesco Totti. Back at Euro 2000, against Holland, just before he went up to take his penalty he told Luigi Di Biagio and Paolo Maldini that he was going to chip the keeper. I made my decision right at the last second, when I saw Joe Hart, the England goalie, doing all sorts on his line. As I began my run-up, I still hadn't decided what I was going to do. And then he moved and my mind was made up. It was all impromptu, not premeditated. The only way I could see of pushing my chances of scoring close to 100%. There was absolutely no showboating about it – that's not my style.

Many so-called experts perceived all manner of hidden meanings in that episode. A secret desire for revenge; something I'd practised again and again on the training pitch between games. Well, for one thing, we hardly trained at all towards the end of that tournament – the constant travelling between joint hosts Poland and Ukraine ate into our time and energy. And anyway, can you really plan something like that so far in advance? If you can, you're either Totti, a clairvoyant or stupid.

Nobody knew I was going to strike the ball like that, simply because I didn't know myself. I'm aware that this explanation will make some people unhappy and make others seem like liars, but the fact is the truth's a lot less romantic than how it may have looked. It was pure calculation that made me chip the ball. At that precise instant, it was the least dangerous thing to do. The safest and most productive option.

In many people's eyes, it was a nice way to win against opponents who had started out as favourites. A nice way to turn what had looked like defeat into victory and to go from almost being knocked out to qualifying for the semi-finals. But the whole thing came and went in a very short space of time, or at least it did for me; my team-mates declared themselves astonished and wanted to dig deeper.

At first they congratulated me, and then immediately asked the question they all had in their heads. They were a children's choir made up of adults who'd apparently lost their minds. Their doubt was almost existential: "Are you mad, Andrea?"

They were amazed, but I was not. I knew why I'd done it. And for how many people.

10 Italy beat France on penalties to win the final of the 2006 World Cup in Berlin after the game ended 1-1. Pirlo was named in the FIFA team of the tournament after finishing up with a goal and three assists in Germany.

Chapter 6

It's no coincidence that such overwhelming emotions come from wearing the Italy shirt. Blue's the colour of the sky, and the sky belongs to everyone. Even when it's covered by clouds, you still know it's there.

After the World Cup in Brazil in 2014, I'll retire from international football. I'll be hanging up my heart. Until that day, nobody must dare ask me to stop, apart from Cesare Prandelli, should he have tactical reasons. I'll be 35 by then, and it'll be time to give someone else a go. I'll probably not feel as useful as I do now and have done in the past – but, to be clear, that day hasn't arrived just yet.

Being part of a team that belongs to everyone makes me feel good and at peace with myself. It relaxes me. A lot of the time, it's better than sex: it lasts longer and if it all falls flat, it can't just be your fault.

Take someone like Antonio Cassano. He says he's slept with 700 women in his time, but he doesn't get picked for Italy any more. Deep down, can he really be happy? I certainly wouldn't be. That second skin, with its smurf-like blue, gives you a whole new image across the world. It makes you better, takes you to a higher level. Much better to be a soldier on the pitch than in the bedroom.

The moment the first bars of the national anthem *Inno di Mameli* ring out, you're representing everyone – a soloist becoming part of an orchestra. And, in theory, you should never say goodbye to the national team; it should always be a coach taking the decision for you. That would make things that little bit sweeter and a whole lot less complicated.

Apart from a few friendlies, no club I've played for has ever put any pressure on me to turn down an Italy call-up. Probably because they know fine well what the response would be – not a particularly polite one. I think that if it did happen, I'd act on instinct and go against the wishes of the directors. Italy is simply more important. More important than Inter, Milan, Juventus or any other club side. It's the biggest deal there is.

I find it really irritating when we're in camp at Coverciano and it's obvious that clubs are looking after their own interests. Remembering Italy only when there's a World Cup or European Championship, bringing with it a bandwagon they can always climb aboard if there's success to celebrate. For these people, it's the league, the Coppa Italia and the Champions League that matter; they don't give a toss about anything else except for a month every other year.

This sporadic pride really makes me angry. It wounds me more than people can possibly imagine. Players know that if they get injured with Italy, there'll be trouble waiting for them when they return to their clubs. And yet I'll never rein myself in or take a backwards step – for me, that would be high treason.

My first experience of international football was with Italy's under-15s and, since then, I've never looked back. I've ticked every box along the way. I think of it as a ladder where you can't see the top, but you're well aware of a plaque positioned on the bottom rung: Paradise This Way. To tell the truth, my first experience of that under-15 team was a little bit unlawful. I didn't meet the minimum age to take part in tournaments, but the selector, Sergio Vatta, called me up anyway for a spot of work experience.

We could have forged the documents, but that's not the right thing to do even if, a few years later, a similar ruse was considered to allow me to play in the Brescia reserves. It's funny – women knock a few years off their age, but people always seem to want to make me older.

I was happy to receive a call-up because I got three days off school – let's just say that my priorities were different back then. I made up for it later on, with catch-up courses undertaken in person: travelling the world with Italy (geography), winning (history), running (PE), getting to know Guardiola (philosophy, art history, and languages: not Spanish but definitely Catalan).

I'm a lucky boy. The shirt I wear has a rare prestige and it's the team I've always supported. I'm what you'd call an Italy *ultra*[11]. I can only just recall Mexico 1986, but I remember every last detail of Italia 90. One thing sticks with me in particular: the theme tune, *An Italian Summer*, sung by Edoardo Bennato and Gianna Nannini ("Maybe a song won't change the rules of the game/but I want to live the adventure just like this/without boundaries and with my heart in my mouth.")

For footballers of my generation, it's both a hymn to joy

and a battle cry. In Germany in 2006, we all had it on our iPods. Some guys were still listening to it at Euro 2012: it's a song that's always current, even after 22 years, just like the ones penned by Lucio Battisti[12]. He's immortal, and so are the emotions he brings out in you.

Some of the bonds you forge in camp also have that timeless quality. They're true, pure friendship. Room 205 at Coverciano, spartan as it is with its two single beds, a little bathroom and tiny terrace, has been a chamber of secrets for me. First I shared it with Alessandro Nesta, and then with Daniele De Rossi, the two extremes of Roman football. Sandrino is a heartfelt *Laziale* and Daniele a committed *Romanista*, but in Germany they were united in internal torment that proved difficult to deal with.

We tried together; just us three. Nesta got injured straight away, against the Czech Republic in the group stage. Lots of tears and tension followed – he was worn out and refused to speak to anyone apart from Daniele and I. Lippi occasionally gave us the night off and we'd take him out for dinner, trying everything we could to distract him and lift his spirits, but he kept repeating the same phrase: "I don't feel part of this team; I'm always getting injured."

On one occasion, we were coming back by car from Dusseldorf, the closest city to our base in Duisburg. Sandrino was driving, with me, Daniele and Andrea Barzagli also in the vehicle. We were on the motorway when, out of the blue, first me and then Daniele shouted out the same thing: "You're going the wrong way; you've got to come off here at Ausfahrt."

"What?"

"Seriously, Sandrino, take the exit!"

"You sure?"

"Of course we are. You've got to come off right here, otherwise we'll end up getting back late and have to pay a fine."

To follow our instructions, Sandrino pulled off a quite audacious manoeuvre. A hundred miles an hour to zero in the space of five seconds, a stamp on the brakes followed by a huge swerve towards a hairpin bend. Naturally enough, we ended up in a ghostly spot with no lights, surrounded by fields that looked like they'd been taken straight out of *Children of the Corn*, the worst film I've ever seen. We were lost. Daniele and I were killing ourselves laughing, but Nesta was all worried. "What the fuck are you laughing about? How are we going to get back now?"

"Sandrino…"

"Fuck me; it's bad enough that I have to read in the papers every day that I'm losing it. Now they're going to write that I'm the first Italy player to go missing in action during a World Cup."

"Sandrino…"

"Where the fuck are we?"

"Sandrino…"

"Will you stop laughing? What do you want?"

"Sandrino, *ausfahrt* means exit in German."

The only reason he didn't beat us to within an inch of our lives was because he'd have ended up with an injured arm as well. He certainly wanted to. I didn't think it was humanly possible for someone to swear as much as he did that night, but we'd achieved our goal: for a few hours he'd thought about something else and managed to enjoy himself.

He held up pretty well until a few days before the semifinal against Germany in Dortmund. In training, he'd undergone a fitness test to see how he was. If he'd really healed, there was a definite possibility he could get back out on the pitch. At a certain point he raised his leg just a little, and was instantly struck by the terrible realisation that something had gone.

He was dying inside and we weren't much better, having seen the effort he'd put into sustaining a hope that was now extinguished. He managed to hold it together in front of Lippi and the rest of the squad, but back in his room it was a different story. I'm not sure anyone has ever cried as many tears all in one go. He didn't want people seeing him like that, and, knowing him as I do, I believe it took a superhuman effort to avoid the collapse taking place in public.

When a dream dies like that, there's no way of striking back. You take the punch and suffer the consequences. Physical ones, yes, but more than anything they're psychological.

Daniele wasn't having a much better time of it. Everyone remembers the elbow on Brian McBride in the game against the United States[13]. What the fans don't know (apart from a few guilty ones) is that in camp, my team-mate started to receive menacing letters, insults and threats against his family. There were some awful things directed at his parents, two absolute diamonds.

Every day there was post for him. The postman always rings twice, but if we were expecting to see Maria De Filippi[14] on the doorstep, it turned out to be Hannibal Lecter, standing there with poison pen letters in his hand. Daniele took it all really badly. I remember long periods, whole days in fact, when he didn't want to see another soul.

Anyone who knows him will tell you he's got a massive heart, something that actually makes things worse when you're in such a bad place.

Sometimes he'd come up to us and whisper: "Sandro, Andrea, how's it going?" A banal little question thrown out there to let us know that he was going mad; that his desire to unburden himself was heading off the scale.

A four-match ban is long enough under normal circumstances. When you're playing a World Cup, it's a prison sentence. You realise you're running the risk of never getting out of there.

We, his team-mates, weren't exactly the most tactful to begin with. "Daniele, what the fuck have you done?" we asked him. We knew we were losing one of our most important assets. Almost immediately, though, friendship got the upper hand. Mates are there to be cared for, not questioned. You love them regardless.

The letters didn't stop arriving, but they polluted things less and less. De Rossi came back and scored a penalty in the final, a nice reply with return receipt to all those classless scribblers. Judging by the spelling and grammar mistakes that cropped up in between the insults, they lacked intellect as well as dignity.

I was happy to help Daniele, and now it's his turn to have my back on the pitch as well. Every time I see him, I tell him the same thing. "Dero, I'm going to retire from international football after the 2014 World Cup. And I want to play in the final again."

It's a pity that Sandrino can't be there. He got off at Ausfahrt.

---

11 Ultras are the self-styled most passionate, vocal and committed supporters of a team. Although the term can have negative connotations, it is not synonymous with 'hooligans'

12 A leading figure on the Italian rock/pop scene in the 1970s and 80s. Died in 1998, but his songs remain popular

13 After beating Ghana 2-0 in their opening group fixture (with Pirlo scoring and being named Man of the Match), Italy took the lead against USA through Alberto Gilardino. A Cristian Zaccardo own goal saw the States draw level, before De Rossi was sent off for crudely elbowing striker Brian McBride in the face (and drawing blood) as the pair jumped for a high ball. Despite USA suffering two red cards of their own and playing much of the second half with nine men, Italy couldn't force the win, with De Rossi bearing the brunt of the public's ire

14 Maria De Filippi hosts an Italian TV show called C'è Posta per Te (There's post for you)

Chapter 7

At his first press conference as Inter coach, Jose Mourinho surprised everyone by introducing himself in perfect Italian. "I'm no *pirla*[15]," he said.

I, on the other hand, definitely am. Pirla and Pirlo, both the feminine and masculine forms, just to cover all the bases. My two Roman mates, Nesta and De Rossi, would call me a *cazzaro*[16].

My face, with its fixed expression, doesn't let on what I'm thinking. But therein lies the beauty. I can make up the most crazy stories, say the most ridiculous things to my teammates and everyone thinks I'm being deadly serious. They don't realise what's happening and I have a whale of a time. I'll be smiling inside, but outwardly completely impassive as I plot my next joke. And sometimes it's cost me a slap, particularly when Rino Gattuso was around.

With him not being a man of letters, a distinguished orator or a member of the Accademia della Crusca[17], whenever Rino opened his mouth the dressing room turned into the Rio Carnival. People would be blowing raspberries, making trumpet noises, doing the conga. Always the same reaction. We'd never let him finish before we started taking the piss. It was the Maracana at Milanello (or Coverciano), and he'd be speaking Portuguese without even knowing. To be fair, it's the same story with Italian where Rino is concerned.

I'd call him *terrone*[18] and he'd hit me. To get my own back, I'd nick his phone and send a bunch of texts to Ariedo Braida, our general manager. This one time, Rino de Janeiro, like me, was waiting for his contract to be renewed. I did the negotiating on his behalf by means of a single message. "Dear Ariedo, if you give me what I want, you can have my sister."

Rino found out and gave me a beating before ringing up Braida. "It's just one of Pirlo's stupid jokes," he said. I've always wondered if the response was, "what a pity".

Before Italy games, De Rossi would hide under Rino's bed and wait. He'd be there for anything up to half an hour. Gattuso would come in, brush his teeth, stick on his leopard-print pyjamas, get into bed, take out a book and look at the pictures. Just as he was about to fall asleep, Daniele would reach up from under the bed and grab his sides, while I'd burst out of the wardrobe like the worst kind of lover, making horrendous noises. Rino took it really well, despite risking a massive heart attack. First he'd beat up Daniele and then he'd do the same to me. Just to prove he was even handed.

Another time we gave him a soaking with a fire extinguisher. A draw away to the Republic of Ireland had been enough to secure our qualification for the 2010 World Cup in South Africa and so the last group game, against Cyprus in Parma four days later, had become almost like a friendly. Pretty much meaningless, and that's exactly how

we treated it.

Lippi gave us a night off in Florence, and almost all of us went out for dinner. Gattuso didn't – he stayed at the team hotel. When we got back, we were quite drunk, actually very drunk, and we ended up chatting in the lounge. We weren't tired, so we needed to find something to pass the time. Everyone had the same idea: "Let's go and piss off Gattuso."

He was already asleep, with his little nightcap on his head. On the way up the stairs to Rino's room, De Rossi spotted a fire extinguisher. "I'm off to put out Gattuso," he said. We knocked on the door and out Rino came, screwing his eyes up as he advanced. Daniele started spraying, covering him in every last drop before running off to hide in his room (i.e. our room). He left me at the mercy of that monster in its underpants, absolutely dripping with foam and shouting total gibberish. Listening to him, though, I knew he was beginning to wake up and regain his senses. I tried to escape, but I was already done for. When the guy on your shoulder is Gattuso and he's out to do you harm, you can run as hard as you like, but he'll always catch you. You could be a gazelle or a lion – it makes absolutely no difference.

With the door safely locked, De Rossi came over all bold. "What's all this noise? I'm pretty sure I've heard something similar in the Bud Spencer and Terence Hill films." For the record, the noise was Rino running me through his full repertoire of slaps.

He said goodnight and returned to his room. That's how he is: he's either playing or he's back at camp. He doesn't do crazy joy, isn't interested in letting his concentration slide. He just can't bear the thought of having left a stone unturned in the quest to win a game.

He's also superstitious to a pretty disgusting degree. At the 2006 World Cup, because things were going well, he kept the same tracksuit on for more than a month. It was something like 40 degrees in Germany and he was going about dressed like a deep-sea diver. From round about the quarter-finals, he began to stink. Never mind a fire extinguisher – what he really needed was an industrial supply of lavender.

Rino's always been my favourite target, top of the table by some distance. This despite the fact that on several occasions he's tried to kill me with a fork. During meal times at Milanello, we'd invent all sorts to torment him and put him on the spot. When he got his verbs wrong (pretty much the whole time), we'd jump on him immediately. And then when he actually got them right, we'd make out that it was still wrong just to wind him up even more. Me, Ambrosini, Nesta, Inzaghi, Abbiati, Oddo: that was the group of bastards right there.

"Rino, how are you?"

"Bad. We got beat yesterday. I was better if we won."

"Rino, try again. It's 'I'd be better if we'd won'."

"But it's the same thing."

"Not exactly, Rino."

"Fine then. I'd be better if we'd won."

"Rino, just how ignorant are you? 'I was better if we won.' That's how you say it."

"But that's what I said before."

"What, Rino?"

"That thing about winning."

"What thing, Rino? Can you repeat it?"

You could see the red mist coming down and he just

wasn't able to hide it. We could tell what was coming and so we'd commandeer all the knives. Gattuso would grab a fork and try to stick it in us. On more than one occasion, he struck his intended target and the fork sank into our skin. We were as soft as tuna; the kind you can cut with a breadstick. Some of us ended up missing games because of one of Rino's fork attacks, even if the official explanation from the club was one of muscle fatigue.

We'd get out of his way when he got mad but once he'd calmed down and gone to his room, we'd come back out, pile up the sofas in front of the door and block his exit.

"Let me out – training starts in a while."

"Deal with it, *terrone*."

He'd then go crazy again, smashing up everything in sight. But even when he was angry, he was one of the good guys. I've always thought of him as being like a character from a film by Woody Allen, my favourite director of all time. I picture him with that No.8 shirt, foaming at the mouth as he tries to deliver lines like: "I will not eat oysters. I want my food dead. Not sick. Not wounded. Dead." Or: "There's nothing wrong with you that can't be cured with a little Prozac and a polo mallet."

Amongst other things, I've seen Rino catch and eat live snails for a bet. He really does belong in a film. I like to think of myself as a director, on the pitch and in life, and I'd never let an actor of his class pass me by.

You need pillars like him in the dressing room. Bodies get older but charisma doesn't age. You run less, but you count for more, in terms of personality. Rino's word was law at Milan, and anyone new to the club was aware that the first thing they'd have to do if they made a mistake was explain themselves to him. Just having that knowledge drastically reduced the chances of people fucking up. Back in the day, that's how things worked, and even old Woody wouldn't have been able to change the ending all that much.

Once upon a time, teams had players who were the very symbol of that club. Standard bearers. And clubs would make a point of holding onto every piece of the flag: the pole, the rope, the fabric, the prestige, the ability to catch the wind and, in some exceptional cases, make it change direction and intensity. Nowadays, the only thing that counts is saving money. It's about cutting salaries that those same clubs had agreed.

When a club throws a tantrum, leaving out a player who's refusing to take a wage cut, people often react on instinct. They'll pass instant judgment: "Aah, typical rich guy, won't let a single penny go. We normal folk go hungry and they want to hang on to their millions. They're the real untouchables in this country; worse than politicians, that lot. What a bunch of tight gits they are: the more they have, the more they want."

When I hear certain understandable gut reactions of that kind, a few questions come to mind. They're not in any particular order, and I don't know how intelligent they are, but here goes: did the directors have a gun to their head when they agreed that multi-million euro salary? Might it be the case that once they realised they'd got their sums wrong, they blamed it all on the player, always an easy sacrificial lamb?

How do people outside the dressing room know whether a player has to provide for a large family, give something back to parents who've made sacrifices for him in the past or pay off debts for relatives and friends? Are you telling me that the big cheeses, after organising all kinds of clandestine dinners and secret meetings to get a player to their club and then showering him with gold, can suddenly ask for it all back? Are they not the liars, those guys who, when it came down to it, weren't capable of keeping their word? How can an employer change at will the terms of a contract that he himself set out?

It's undeniable that we footballers are a fortunate bunch. But we've got our dignity. And at least from that point of view, nobody can call us *pirlas*.

---

15 Term used in the Milan/Lombardy dialect roughly translating as 'dickhead'. Can be used quasi-affectionately

16 Term used in the Roman dialect to mean 'stupid'

17 An organisation that seeks to preserve the purity of the Italian language

18 An offensive term meaning 'peasant' used by northern Italians against southerners

Chapter 8

I consider myself particularly fortunate: I know Antonio Conte. I've worked with a lot of coaches in my time, and he's the one who surprised me the most. One little speech, a few simple words, was all it took for him to win me over. Me and the whole of Juventus, a planet we disembarked on pretty much at the same time.

On the first day of our training camp up in the mountains at Bardonecchia, he got everyone together in the gym to introduce himself. He had some venom ready for us and the altitude wasn't causing him any trouble. I suppose that's just how vipers roll.

"Lads, we've finished seventh each of the last two seasons. Crazy stuff; absolutely appalling. I've not come here for that. It's time we stopped being crap."

After only a few minutes, he'd stripped away all the mystery. One thing in particular was very obvious: he was like a bear with a sore head. As we Italians say, *'Aveva un diavolo per capello'* – 'he'd a devil for hair', and if the hair was fake then the devil was 100% real and made from a material that's impossible to replicate.

"Every single person here has performed badly over the last few seasons. We need to do whatever it takes to pull ourselves up and start being Juve again. Turning round this ship is not a polite request; it's an order, a moral obligation. You guys need to do only one thing and it's pretty simple: follow me."

Our first impression was absolutely correct. When Conte speaks, his words assault you. They crash through the doors of your mind, often quite violently, and settle deep within you. I've lost track of the number of times I've found myself saying: "Hell, Conte said something really spot-on again today."

"And listen carefully, boys, because I'm not finished. Get it into your heads that we must return to the levels where we belong, the ones that are written into the history of this club. It would be criminal for us not to finish in the top three this year."

Naturally we won the *scudetto* at the first time of asking[19] and it was all down to him. The success was all his, a triumph of bloody mindedness that went beyond everyone's expectations. It really couldn't have gone any other way, given the example we had in front of us every day. Conte was like a man possessed, the very essence of Juventus burned deep into his soul.

"You all need the same anger as me. Full stop." His message was short and to the point, a bit like a telegram – certainly the most convincing one that I've ever received. He's not a guru, Conte, nor is he a magician, for all he's been known to pull some crazy speeches out of the hat. You either do what he says or you don't play. He runs on Conte-time and so do we.

He obsesses over every last detail, exploiting it to his advantage. When he's looking at tactics, he'll have us watching videos for hours, explaining over and over again where and why we got a move wrong. He's plainly allergic to error (perhaps to horror as well) and I for one pray every day that a cure is never found.

Out on the training pitches at Vinovo, quite often we'll end up winning, for the simple reason that we're not playing against anyone. From Monday to Friday, the opposition don't exist. He'll have us playing games of 11 versus none, making us repeat the same moves for three-quarters of an hour, until he sees they're working and that we're starting to feel sick.

And that's why we still win when it's 11 against 11. If Arrigo Sacchi was a genius, then what does that make Conte? I was expecting him to be good, but not *this* good. I thought he'd be a tough, committed, charismatic kind of coach, but plenty of other managers could learn a lot from him in terms of his technical and tactical awareness.

If I could go back in time, I'd change only one thing: I wouldn't pick the spot next to Buffon in our dressing room. It's the one right in front of the door, and the most dangerous spot in the whole of Turin, especially at half-time. Even when we're winning, Conte comes in and hurls against the wall (and thus my little corner) anything he can lay his hands on, almost always full bottles of water. Fizzy water. Very fizzy water.

It's really quite a rage. He's never happy – there's always some small detail that's not quite right in his mind. He can see in advance what might happen in the 45 minutes still to come. This one time, for instance, we were losing to Milan and he just couldn't make sense of it. "Losing to them! Them! I can't understand why we're not beating them! They're not even playing well!"

It's a different story at the end of a match: he tends to disappear completely. At a push, he'll come in for a quick word, but only if we've won. He's at his worst at night when he's alone with his thoughts. He necks these horrible concoctions to help him sleep, almost like he's actually just played the game. He was the exact same when he did play. He struggles to sleep and goes over and over everything, then hits the rewind button in his head and does it all again.

It's an inner torment without a start or end point, a song on some kind of loop where you can't tell what's the first verse and what's the last, you can only make out the chorus. He's completely immersed in his job, which is also his great pleasure. I've never quite understood whether it's the coach or the fan who takes up position in the dugout, but either way it's someone who makes a difference.

He still managed to have that effect even during the long ban linked to the strange *Calcioscommesse* affair, dating back to his time at Siena[20]. You could tell he really felt it on a Wednesday, Saturday and Sunday – those are the most important days for the team and he wasn't allowed to come near us. It drove him absolutely crazy that he couldn't pop his head into the dressing room (let's just say he ended up there a few times by mistake).

His absence was obvious at half-time, but his deputies, Angelo Alessio and Massimo Carrerra, simply did what he'd told them to. They didn't have much freedom in the post-match interviews either: Conte supplied the ideas and words, and they put their faces to them.

I never once saw him cry or get upset during that whole period. Just before the sentence was delivered, we were out at a training camp in China and the tension was writ large on his face. He was spending whole days on the phone to his lawyers. He never went into specifics with us players; he was good at keeping us separate from his problems and making out that nothing had changed.

Only on one occasion, just before the bomb went off, did he ask the leaders for help. I was there, along with Buffon, Giorgio Chiellini and Claudio Marchisio. "Lads, this is a difficult time. You need to give me a hand, even more so than normal. Give your all in training and in the games and when I'm not there, you be the ones who keep the rest of the boys on their toes. Don't slacken off. Don't let everything we've built go to hell in a handcart."

We felt really sorry for him and his assistant Cristian Stellini, who ended up leaving the club. He'd been a big part of the group and spent a lot of time with us players. He looked after the defensive side of our game and when he left, we really felt his absence. One night he came into my hotel room after a friendly we'd played down in Salerno. It was 3am. "Andrea, I can't stay here any more," he said. "I'm leaving, because I love Juventus and I want to calm the waters."

One thing I know for sure. The real problem lies in official, authorised betting. Ever since that's been legalised, the whole thing has got worse. It's provided a really dangerous springboard for those prone to taking things too far and for those who want to involve themselves in dodgy, shady affairs.

For me, the authorities should take a drastic decision with regards to Serie B and Serie C: make it impossible to bet on those leagues. Particularly in Serie C (or rather, Lega Pro, because that's what it's called even if nobody remembers). There are players who haven't been paid in weeks. So they make an agreement amongst themselves to manipulate the result, place a bet at the bookies and manage to get by until the end of the month. Then until the end of the year. Then until who knows when. And it's not much better in Serie B.

I'm sure people will object and say that if official betting didn't exist, the schemes run by the Mafia, Camorra and other similar nasty pieces of work would simply take their place. That's certainly a possibility, but let's sort out one problem and then throw ourselves into the next. Not taking that first step makes the second one impossible.

Personally, I think that any player caught with their hand in the till should be struck off there and then. No second chances for those who steal and play hide and seek all at the same time. I just don't know what goes on in some people's heads, including so-called champions. For me, it's an illness to always want more money when you've already got infinite riches.

Nobody has ever tried to involve me in anything, and in that respect it was a blessing to spend so many years at Milan. Losing and drawing simply don't enter the equation there. You go out with a single thought in your head: winning. If anyone had ever tried to get me involved in shit like that, I would have kicked them into the middle of next week. I'm not normally a violent man, but don't push me.

And, yes, we can all appear blind and deaf. In Serie B all sorts of crazy stuff goes on, especially towards the end of the season. There are some really surreal games and nobody ever says a word. No player has ever stuck their head above the parapet. There are whispers that even in Serie A, certain teams will allow themselves to be led by the hand, so to speak. The really difficult step for a player to take is reporting a fellow pro who tries to involve him in a fix. What do you do? Especially if he's a team-mate or, worse still, a friend. You tell him 'no' and have a go at him. If it were me, I'd probably give him a good slap. But how on earth do you then go and tell the authorities that he was about to commit the mother of all mistakes? At that point, they're going to train the spotlight on you, too, even though you've nothing to do with it. You could end up paying the price for an attempted fraud despite having absolutely no guilt.

That's why I believe the principle of collective responsibility is wrong in this sort of case. You mess up, you involve me, I tell you 'no', I insult you, I don't report you, and now they can come after me as well. It just doesn't stack up.

In addition to getting rid of betting, there should be incentives for winning. I'll give you an example of how it might work. Team B are second in the league and up against Team C, who don't have anything much to play for. If Team B lose, Team A (currently top of the table) go on to win the league. So Team A approach Team C and say: "Here's some money. It's yours if you beat Team B."

With positive incentives like that, every team would fight right until the finish without any sort of subterfuge. It already happens abroad, but I fear that in Italy we'll never arrive at a similar solution because there are too many interests at stake. And that's something I'm willing to bet on.

Chapter 8

19 Juventus won the 2011-12 Serie A title by four points, going the entire league
    season unbeaten

20 Calcioscommesse was a match fixing/betting scandal that saw Antonio Conte
    banned for 10 months, reduced to four on appeal

Chapter 9

I wouldn't bet a single cent on me becoming a manager, though. It's not a job I'm attracted to. There are too many worries and the lifestyle is far too close to that of a player. I've done my bit and, in the future, I'd like to get back even a semblance of a private life. There's only one Antonio Conte and that's fine by me, even if Marcello Lippi wasn't too dissimilar when he got pissed off.

It was a real team effort that made us world champions in Germany but, at one point, Lippi had this to say about the group: "You're all shits; you disgust me." Before our quarter-final against Australia, a game we won thanks to a (non-existent) Francesco Totti penalty, he called us into a meeting room at the team hotel and tore us all to shreds.

"You talk to the journalists too much. You're spies who can't keep a single secret – those guys always know the team in real time. What's that all about? I can't even trust you." He wouldn't let us say a word; it was an absolute monologue. He just couldn't keep a lid on it. His face was contorted with rage, and the veins in his neck were about to explode. His brakes had evidently been tampered with.

"Go fuck yourselves: I don't want anything more to do with you. Bunch of bastards. Bastards and spies." The whole thing lasted five minutes, and when Lippi had finished, a good few of us sought Pippo Inzaghi's reaction out of the corner of our eye.

Lippi was the catalyst for a very special experience and emotion that nobody can ever take away from us. But he's also at the heart of a thought that troubles me from time to time. Whenever I meet him, I remember that had he stayed on as Inter coach, I'd probably have become a standard bearer at the club. A less moustachioed Beppe Bergomi[21]. An Esteban Cambiasso[22] with more hair.

My career would certainly have gone in a very definite direction. Had Lippi been in charge, I'd have stayed at Inter for life[23]. After all, they were my team as a kid, when I was an *ultra* with a dummy. My absolute idol was Lothar Mätthaus. He was the No.10 who scored the goals and inspired the rest – for me, there was nobody better. The time I met him on holiday in Viareggio and got his autograph was for a long while the best and most important day of my life.

After Mätthaus came Roberto Baggio. Just as well I had a big bedroom, so that both their posters would fit on the wall and I didn't have to pick which god to pull down from Mount Olympus.

I was still an Inter fan when I was playing for Brescia, but then I spent some time at the club and my outlook changed somewhat. At the end of season 1997/98 I was in camp with the Italy under-21s when my agent rang. "Andrea, you're moving. We've done a deal with Parma. All you need to do is sign the contract."

I really let myself get carried away with the happiness of the moment, condensing my infinite enthusiasm into a single word: "Okay."

The following morning, I got home and it was suddenly all change once more. My mobile went again – more insistently than usual. "Hi Andrea, it's Tullio. Look, last night the Inter president Moratti phoned Luigi Corioni at Brescia to talk about you. They agreed everything between them in less than 10 minutes. You're off to play for the team you love. You're an Inter player – you've done it! Now go and get ready; we need to take you to Appiano Gentile for your medical." There followed another explosion of joy, even more powerful than the first one: "Okay, no worries."

I might not have looked it, but I was the happiest man alive, proud of having thrown myself into the world shown in those posters. I wanted to stick myself up on that wall. I was going to be a team-mate of Ronaldo, Baggio, Djorkaeff – me, the guy who now and again still went to games with a black-and-blue scarf round his neck and who, at 16 years of age, had been invited to play a trial match in Eindhoven by the top men at the club, people like Sandro Mazzola[24].

I played a lot in my first season at Inter. Pre-season went really well, and Gigi Simoni gave me plenty of game time, both as a starter and from the bench. Mircea Lucescu tended to favour the older guys, Luciano Castellini thought I was okay, while Roy Hodgson mispronounced my name. He called me *Pirla* (dickhead), perhaps understanding my true nature more than the other managers.

Moratti went through four of them that season[25]. It was during this time I started to suffer from migraines and sudden memory loss. I'd wake up in the morning and not remember who my coach was. I'd still be smiling, in blissful ignorance. Confused, but grinning.

The following year, they brought in Lippi. I did the full pre-season under him, but he then pulled me aside to give me a heartfelt message. "Andrea, for your own good, you need to go and play somewhere else, at least for a season. Get some experience under your belt. It'll stand you in good stead, you'll see."

I ended up at Reggina, and I did indeed learn a lot. In particular, how to take on more responsibility, and how to get stuck in and fight in the mud.

At the start of season 2000/01, I went back to Inter. Lippi was still there, but he didn't last much longer, barely a single game. I missed that trip to Reggio Calabria through injury, but his post-match press conference has gone down in history. "If I was president Moratti, I'd sack the coach and give the players a good kick up the arse." He got his way, at least with half of that recommendation. Our buttocks remained blissfully untouched.

It was a shame he left, because he and I were very much on the same wavelength. We could understand each other instantly, despite the fact we'd only just met. All it took was one look for me to trust him blindly. It was a real pleasure to work with him.

In his place arrived Marco Tardelli, the former manager of the Italy under-21s. We'd won the European Championship together, but perhaps he didn't recognise me. Whatever the explanation, he never picked me and it really got me down. I lost count of the number of times I wanted to say to him, "you know where you can stick that roar that made you famous" but, being a well-mannered person, I always stopped myself in time.

I no longer had any desire to be near him or that club. He killed it for me, wiping out what could have been a love without limits. I had to escape and, as ever, I got on the phone to Tinti.

"Take me away from this madhouse. I'm done with Inter, for good. Never, ever again. Find me another club. Any club."

I went back to Brescia, on loan for six months, and then I moved to Milan for 12 billion lire[26] plus Andres Guglielminpietro. Who do you reckon got the better of that deal? I don't like speaking ill of anyone, and that includes Tardelli, but the fact is he never gave me a chance. Every now and then he'd say: "I'm doing it for your own good; I don't want you to burn out", but it always seemed like an excuse. Back when he was coaching the under-21s, he said that youngsters were the future.

Had Lippi stayed on, I'd be telling you a different story. The same one brought out every so often by the guy under the next parasol along from me on the beach each summer. "Andrea, you know that if I could go back in time…"

I do know: he'd chain me to the walls of the dressing room at Appiano Gentile. My next door neighbour on the sand is none other than president Moratti. Leaving him behind was the one thing that saddened me when I moved. He's a fantastic person, the exact same as he appears on TV. He's the head of a family, a stately figure in an unseemly world, a slice of goodness in a sea of sharks. He's also a fan, an extremely passionate one, and if that passion has often caused him to make the wrong decision, it can't be considered a fault. If only all presidents were like him.

He does everything in his power to make his club great. It belonged to his father Angelo before him, and theirs is a dynasty of poets, of romantics, of people who still have a heart when they win. Just as importantly, they also have a heart when they lose. I still care about him a lot and always will. I know for certain that the feeling is mutual. Every time I see him, he pays me a thousand compliments. I appreciate them because they're genuine. It's thanks to him that I've never managed to consider Inter an enemy, whether I've been playing for Juventus or Milan. In simple terms, my time at Inter just didn't start or finish as I'd have wanted.

During those long periods when it seemed my world was spinning in the wrong direction, my friends gave me some excellent advice. "When you can't go on, think of something that relaxes you." It turned out to be a precious tip. Whenever I was on the bench, or worse, in the stand, I'd close my eyes for a few seconds and picture myself with my bare feet (no studs, no socks, no shin guards and most of all no pressure) immersed in an enormous wooden barrel.

I was crushing grapes, dancing right on top of them. Pulling down the vines and turning fruit into wine. I thought back to my childhood days spent harvesting the grapes at my grandmother Maria's farm out in the countryside near Brescia. It was me against the grape skins, fighting to save the juice. It's the first metaphor that comes to mind if I have to explain the difference between good and bad; between the useful and the pointless. These were barefoot family reunions, with loads of relatives helping alongside me.

Perhaps it was during those flights of fancy, those daydreams that allowed me to still feel alive, that I learned to appreciate certain alcoholic drinks. Even now, I'll sometimes come home after training, light the fire and pour myself a glass of wine. On our days off, I'll stick on my Juventus tracksuit and go for a run amongst the vines. Where the farm once stood you'll now find Pratum Coller, my father's business. The house specialities are red, white and rosé, and we're also dipping a toe into the world of sparkling wine.

We'll certainly make a saving on tasters: I'll take care of that side of things, and not just because the 'Pirlo' is the most famous Brescia *aperitivo* going. The ingredients are simple: sparkling white wine, Campari and tonic water.

I started drinking it during my time at Inter. Or at least that's what people say.

21 A stalwart of the Inter and Italy defence in the 1980s and 1990s, one-club man Bergomi was known as lo zio (the uncle) because of the prodigious facial hair he sported from an early age

22 Inter's long-serving Argentina midfielder. Always has a shaven head

23 As it was, he left for Milan in 2001 having been contracted to Inter for three years

24 Key figure in the Grande Inter team that enjoyed sustained success under the charismatic Helenio Herrera in the 1960s

25 Season 1998/99

26 Around £9.6m

Chapter 10

I've allowed myself a few good blowouts in my time. The type of seriously heavy session that almost makes you want to dig out that Inter scarf (or Milan pen), look at yourself in the mirror and see a tall, beautiful blond guy with blue eyes staring back.

The perfect moment to let your hair down is usually after a triumph, because defeats deserve a different kind of reaction. Something less pleasant than a drink among team-mates; something far removed from a group toast. As a general rule, I'm more lucid when things go badly. When you lose, it's all about thinking and reflecting. When you win, burping takes priority.

The Ballon d'Or presentation ceremony is the exception that proves the rule. It's the most prestigious individual honour, I never win, and yet I can't bring myself to get upset. They always give it to someone else and I just shrug my shoulders.

In 2012, hot on the heels of reaching the final of the European Championship and winning the *scudetto*, I came seventh with 2.66% of the vote. Practically nothing. Messi won, with 41.6%, and then came Ronaldo (the other one), Iniesta, Xavi, Falcao and Casillas.

I'm fine with that. There's absolutely no doubt that Messi is No.1 and, as such, it was the right result. Over time I've realised that the managers, captains and journalists on the international judging panel all have a soft spot for goalscorers. As a consequence, when it comes to voting they've a preference for strikers, who are considered more influential than their team-mates. There are, of course, some rare exceptions, like King Cannavaro in 2006.

It seems the most important thing is to find yourself in the right place at the right time with the ball at your feet. The assist is a mere footnote. Without the final pass there wouldn't be a goal, but I don't get angry if people forget that fact when they fill in their ballot paper.

Prandelli and Buffon voted for me, but even I would have gone with the majority and chosen Messi. Granted he's got people around him who run and sweat in his place, happy to serve those they know are simply better, but to perform at that sort of level for so many years is beyond every other human being.

As long as he and Cristiano Ronaldo are around, it's a two-horse race. I'm now certain that winning the Ballon d'Or is a bridge too far for me. It's a target I'll never reach and I've come to terms with that.

I don't even properly watch the awards ceremony, even if it's only once a year and I could really make the effort. I'll have Sky Sports on in the background and get on with other stuff. The time I finished seventh, I could hear FIFA president Sepp Blatter rambling on in the distance. The same guy whose self-evident dislike for Italy had led him to delegate what he considered the horrible task of presenting us with the World Cup in 2006. He was speaking from the stage of the Kongresshaus in Zurich while I played football with my son Niccolò in Turin.

"Daddy, over here, they're about to say who's won."

"Okay."

We carried on knocking the ball around, even though the fateful moment was getting closer.

"Come on Daddy, let's go and watch on the TV."

"Okay."

"Hurry, hurry."

"Okay, fine."

We were wasting our time. I really couldn't have cared less about what they were about to reveal. It could have been the fourth secret of Fatima or the first of Blatter. We didn't sit down to hear the results; we stayed firmly on our feet. Truth be told, Niccolò paid much more attention than me, grabbing the remote control and turning up the volume.

"Messi won."

"What a surprise."

It was an inevitable, inarguable result. It crossed my mind that the World Cup and Champions League are worth a lot more than the Ballon d'Or, but I didn't say it out loud. Otherwise I'd have had to add that I've won both while Messi hasn't managed the World Cup yet. I'd have come across as an arrogant snob and that's something I'm really not.

"Ronaldo came second."

"Really?"

"Iniesta third."

A few months previously, Iniesta had been named player

of Euro 2012. Before the final against Spain, the guys from UEFA had blabbed to me that "you're the best, but we'll only give you the award if Italy win". Needless to say we lost 4-0.

"Daddy, Daddy, Falcao fifth, Casillas sixth. And Pirlo, Pirlo! That's you Dad!"

"You're right."

"You came seventh, ahead of Drogba, Van Persie and even Ibrahimovic."

"Come on, let's keep playing."

The headline news was that the first two places had both gone to forwards. Very much in keeping with how the wider world ranks the importance of different positions. The really big mistake that some club presidents make is not realising that it's a different story when it comes to building teams.

Big name collector cards sell season tickets, but it's the glue they have behind them that wins games. The defence is the most important part of a team: in military terms, success starts in the zone behind the lines. Put more simply, the team that concedes fewest goals wins the match.

In terms of pure technical ability, Ronaldo (the real one) is the most gifted guy I've had the pleasure of playing with. He was an absolute machine. But overall, Paolo Maldini is the best. A defender. A peerless defender. The best defender going.

Both physically and mentally, he had everything, and the enjoyment he got from playing was as obvious at 40 years of age as it had been the day I first walked through the door at Milan. His passion is an example and an inspiration, a compass that I'll carry with me not just for the rest of my playing days, but for the rest of my life. No cardinal points;

just points in the league table.

He taught me how to conduct myself. Taught me how to win, lose, sniff out a goal, come up with an assist, sit on the bench, suffer, celebrate, play, behave, get angry, forgive, turn the other cheek, land the first blow, be myself and sometimes someone else. Showed me how to stay quiet, speak, decide, trust, turn a blind eye, have both eyes wide open, take stock of a situation, act on instinct, stand on my own, welcome others in, be the captain, steer the ship, change course, lead the way. Everything and the opposite of everything. Maldini is himself, but he's also a part of me. And not seeing him at Milan after he retired, even as a director, really got to me. How can you possibly decide not to hang onto a piece of your heritage? What makes you stick him on the market and risk losing him like that?

I've no answer because there isn't one. We're still good friends and, as such, we've talked a fair bit about what went on. It's no secret he and Galliani didn't see eye to eye from the moment problems arose in his contract renewal negotiations. Mr Bic offered a one-year deal and Paolo wasn't having it: he felt hard done by and diminished. Not offering him a role that was worthy of him (and we're not even talking something massively glamorous) was like biting off part of his being. It was Tyson against Holyfield and, as usual, it was the bald guy who won. It doesn't seem to matter if he's the one doing the biting or being bitten.

Billy Costacurta is another man I have a great relationship with. He and Paolo were a dual reference point for everyone at Milan, whatever the situation. It could be something stupid: what shoes should I wear? I'll ask Costacurta. Which tie goes better? I'll ask Maldini. What's my best position? I'll ask them both. How should one behave at the dinner table? I'll ask both of them again.

Sometimes, particularly back in the early days, we'd ask them stuff simply for the pleasure of having their attention. They'd talk and we'd win – there was a magic in the air that anyone who came near could feed off. It was just like Christmas, when all you need to feel involved is to hear Jingle Bells and see some old guy dressed as Santa Claus. Suddenly Christmas belongs to you as well.

Over the years, Milan have had Franco Baresi, Mauro Tassotti, Nesta and Thiago Silva in defence. Truly outstanding players; human shields to protect against the errors of others. If a forward makes a mistake, he can try again. If he scores, he's in with a shout of the Ballon d'Or. But when it's a defender who slips up, it's a far more delicate situation. In percentage terms, the people who play at the back make fewer mistakes than those further forward. If not, games would end up 5-4, 6-5 or along those lines. Let's discount teams coached by Zeman[27], because we're talking the very limits of reality there.

While Milan had defenders like those guys, they could do as they wished. They could stick anyone up front. One collector card was the same as the next one.

If I was a president, I'd never build a team with champions up front and dummies in defence. That's just deceitful advertising designed to fool the fans.

---

27 Zdeněk Zeman, the much-travelled Czech-Italian football coach famed for his adventurous, perhaps cavalier, approach to the game

Chapter 11

"Andrea, we've signed this guy Huntelaar so you've got to stay."

Silvio Berlusconi smiled as he handed me a bit of paper he'd just pulled from his trolley case. It was a page crammed full of statistics along with a photo of a blond bloke: the lowdown on the new striker he'd just signed for Milan.

The Pen Guy was sitting beside him, staring intently at me in the hope of spying a positive reaction. It was just the three of us in Milanello's hall with the hearth, even if everyone outside knew that we were in there.

Here's the deal: Klass-Jan Huntelaar is an excellent player. He knows how to score goals, loads of goals and, at that point in time, he was playing for Real Madrid. But he's not the type of guy who's going to win the Ballon d'Or.

"Well then, Andrea lad?"

Our president had a difficult task that day – convincing me to stay. Persuading me to reopen a suitcase that was already on the check-in belt, ready to be weighed and then sent on its way.

It was August 2009 and I'd reached agreement with Chelsea, the club where Ancelotti had just come in as manager. Carlo was like a father and a teacher for me, a kind, friendly man who knew how to make things fun. I'd spent the best years of my career with him. If you're a player who wants to get on and give everything, you won't find anyone better than him.

Ancelotti's even more impressive than Carlo Mazzone back in my Brescia days. You wouldn't see the latter on the training pitch right up until the Thursday. He'd stay in the dressing room, wrapped in a massive jacket out of the cold while his assistant took the session.

Carlo Ancelotti was my motivation for agreeing to head to London. But, in the meantime, Berlusconi had pulled out a second piece of paper. This time there were loads of names with ticks next to them, and one that had been circled.

"Stay. We've signed Huntelaar."

Huntelaar…

"We could have brought in other guys, people like Claudio Pizarro[28], but we chose him."

Huntelaar…

"Listen, Andrea, you just can't do this, damn it. You're the symbol of Milan, a standard bearer for this team, and we've already sold Kaká. You can't jump ship as well. It'd be a terrible blow, to our image as much as anything. We can't have everyone leaving."

During the Confederations Cup that I'd just finished playing, Ancelotti and I spoke a fair bit on the phone, not least because there wasn't much of a time difference between South Africa and England. There was no need to get up at the crack of dawn to hear this particular serenade.

He wanted to bring me to London at all costs, and cost was indeed the last hurdle still to be overcome. Insurmountable, as it transpired. Milan wanted too much cash, and they were also pushing for Branislav Ivanović to be included in the deal. Chelsea hadn't the slightest intention of letting the defender go.

"Mr President, I really like all this talk of being a standard bearer. But my contract here is about to run out, and those guys are offering me four years." At five million euros a season. It wasn't money that had convinced me, more the length of the deal. That's always very important.

"Where's the problem, Andrea? You can sort all that out with Galliani, can't you? Take it as read."

"You sure?"

"Absolutely positive."

No sooner were the words out of his mouth than he shot out of the room to tell the media: "Andrea Pirlo is not for sale. He's staying with Milan and he'll finish his career right here."

As it turned out, I moved to Juventus. That's Berlusconi all over, though. He's theatrical and knows exactly what he wants. It's what makes him such a fantastic president and lover of pure, beautiful football. Winning isn't enough for him.

When he was at his busiest with political commitments, we didn't see that much of him. He'd only come to the really big sold-out games like the Milan derby and when Barcelona or Juventus were in town. He'd go whole years without coming to see us, and we certainly felt his absence, but that was all blown away on the rare occasions when he did drop in.

It's perhaps difficult to understand, and even harder to explain, but whenever we heard the whir of his helicopter at Milanello, it sparked a positive feeling deep within us. We were like abandoned dogs furiously wagging our tails at the return of our master.

Once he was on the ground, he'd speak with the players and soon have us wound up like coiled springs. From that point of view, he'll always be the best; a presidential version of Conte. He'd call us individually into a small room a few metres along from the training pitch. He loved those one-on-ones, and he'd usually spend a little bit of extra time with Inzaghi, whom he also phoned on occasion.

They had a lot to talk about. I, on the other hand, have never taken a call from Berlusconi. I've voted for him in the past, even if he never asked us to directly. Often he'd say that football was sacred and politics profane. Naturally, he'd explain why his plans would make Italy great, and he'd also compare the team's success with the flourishing of his companies. We'd hear him talk about creating a million jobs. Minus one: mine. Every so often, he'd update us on the stats, which proved somewhat different to those of our friend Huntelaar.

Huntelaar...

If he saw that you were interested, he'd go into detail on a topic, like you'd see him do on Bruno Vespa's TV show[29]. And then, out of the corner of his eye, he'd spy that Ancelotti was about to walk past and suddenly he'd break off. "Carlo, son, remember that I want to see the team play with two strikers."

How could he forget? He'd heard it a billion times. He and everyone else.

"Another thing, Carlo. We need to own the pitch and boss the game. In Italy, in Europe, throughout the world."

They'd debate tactics, but the final decision always lay with the coach. If you'll pardon my French, Ancelotti had massive balls. A big guy with a big personality.

He and Berlusconi had a few differences of opinion, in particular towards the end of Carlo's time at Milan, but theirs is an enduring, mutual affection. The same can't be said of certain other coaches, for example the Turk Fatih Terim, whom Ancelotti ended up replacing. He was a remarkable person, a really strange fellow who seemed allergic to rules. It was obvious from an early stage that he wouldn't last long and sure enough he was fired.

Before Milan, he'd been with smaller, less stately clubs who'd allowed him to do as he pleased. The environment was different at Milan. He'd arrive late for lunch, turn up for official engagements without a tie, run off and leave Mr Bic on his own at the table just so he could watch Big Brother. You'd see him walking around Milanello with garishly loud clothes, looking like John Travolta.

He had this mad translator, practically his shadow, who at one point advised him to cut off relations with the media. Indefinitely. At Milan. The club where communication is always *par excellence*.

The translator also had a few problems getting across Terim's message to those of us in the dressing room. The coach would be gesticulating and talking away in Turkish: "Boys, we're about to play one of the most important matches of the season. Lots of people are criticising us, but I believe in you. We can't give up now. There are great expectations upon us, and we've a moral obligation not to disappoint.

Let's do it for ourselves, for the club, for the president, for the fans. There are moments in life when a man has to lift his head. I believe that moment has arrived for us. Go on, boys. *Go on.*"

The translator, standing there quite motionless, would then say in Italian: "Juventus are coming tomorrow. We need to win." One of them spoke for five minutes, the other for five seconds.

Terim: "Andrea, you'll be the focal point for our game. You direct our play, but take your time and don't force it. Weigh up the situation and give the ball to the team-mate who has the fewest opponents around him. We're relying on you: you're absolutely fundamental for this team and the way we want to play. But I'll say it again: don't force it. Calm and cool are the watchwords here. First think, then pass: that's the only way we'll get the right result and show the whole of Italy we're still alive. That we won't go down without a fight. Right, now, everyone out on the pitch. Let's see an amazing session with real intensity. I want it to be right up there with the best we've had this year."

The translator: "Pirlo pass the ball. And now let's go and train."

Some of the team meetings, especially in the early days, were absolutely unforgettable. Terim would stand in front of the tactics board, take out a piece of chalk and draw 11 circles. Each circle represented a player, but it got to the point that there were so many notes and scribbles, you couldn't tell which circles were the defenders, which the midfielders and which the strikers. Total chaos: only the goalkeeper wasn't in doubt.

He'd point to a circle and say: "Okay, Costacurta, you

Rino's always been my favourite target, despite the fact that he tried to kill me with a fork

2005: I thought about quitting because, after Istanbul, nothing made sense any more

2007: We celebrated, but didn't forget

I made my decision right at the last second, when I saw Joe Hart doing all sorts on his line

I spent the afternoon of July 9 2006 sleeping and playing the PlayStation. In the evening, I won the World Cup

With the under-21s at the Olympics. Bronze face, just like my medal

On holiday in Viareggio
with a freshly-bought shirt:
Inter, of course

Finally at Inter and I'm
even smiling

With Italy under-16s in Red Square in Moscow, Russia

At my parents' house. One cool guy, I'm sure you'll agree

Me in my Fiero Juniors shirt. Even back then I wanted to be the one with the ball

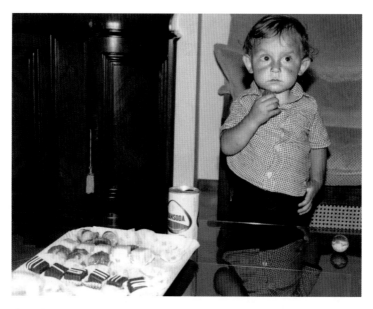

I'm going to eat them all, but don't tell Granny

Want to bet that I'll become a top player?

I've got well-hidden tattoos: my son Niccolò's name in Chinese letters on my neck; an 'A' for his sister Angela just below

Alessandro Nesta: Friend, brother, team-mate, roomie

I tried to copy Juninho's free-kicks and eventually I understood his secret

Each free-kick bears my name and they're all my children

We need Mario Balotelli … he's an antidote to the racists. Whenever I see him, I'll give him a big smile

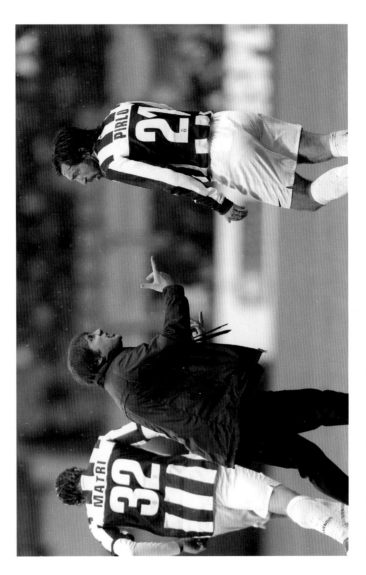

When Conte speaks, his words assault you

The team belongs to Agnelli and to everyone: it's a communist
co-operative at the heart of a capitalist state

need to go here."

And I'd be forced to pipe up: "But boss, that's me." It was even worse when he mistook the defenders for strikers – I began to suspect he was doing it on purpose. Four forwards on the pitch and only two defenders: Berlusconi's forbidden dream.

But even Terim was aware that without the president, that type of president, Milan would have been nothing, both in terms of money and power. Without his cash and commitment, they'd have ended up like lots of other clubs.

Berlusconi would go mad, quite literally, when we won in Europe or on the global stage. He'd burst into song, strum along with his mucker Mariano Apicella[30], tell jokes. Under his command, Milan became the most decorated club in the world, just as it now says beneath the crest on the players' shirts. Berlusconi, by extension, is the most decorated president.

And he signed Huntelaar.

---

28 The Peruvian striker who has scored prolifically for Bayern Munich and Werder Bremen either side of an unsuccessful spell with Chelsea

29 Bruno Vespa is the host of a long-running news and politics programme Porta a Porta (Door to Door) shown on the Italian state-owned channel Rai Uno

30 An Italian singer famous for performing songs written by Berlusconi

Chapter 12

There was a time when I thought about quitting football, but Huntelaar wasn't to blame. I just didn't want to have anything more to do with it – the mere thought turned my stomach. I'd eaten too much already; I was on the verge of throwing up.

It wasn't even the fault of Zlatan Ibrahimovic and Oguchi Onyewu, two of my former team-mates at Milan. One of them is the only mean Swede, the other the solitary American who prefers football to baseball, basketball, gridiron, ice hockey and even hamburgers from McDonald's.

During a training session at Milanello, I saw them laying into one another like two bully boys from the roughest estate. They looked like they were trying to kill each other: there were definitely some broken ribs, despite silence and denials from the king's buglers who said it was just a "lively confrontation".

Those of us who'd witnessed it were put in mind of a Mafia-style settling of the scores. It was like something out of *Highlander* – there can be only one. That pair certainly caused me alarm, but it wasn't them who killed my desire for a footballing future. If anything, they were too busy trying to bump off one another.

I thought about quitting because, after Istanbul, nothing made sense any more. The 2005 Champions League final simply suffocated me[31]. To most people's minds, the reason we lost on penalties was Jerzy Dudek – that jackass of a dancer who took the mickey out of us by swaying about on his line and then rubbed salt into the wound by saving our spot kicks. But in time the truly painful sentence was realising that we were entirely to blame.

How it happened I don't know, but the fact remains that when the impossible becomes reality, somebody's fucked up – in this case, the entire team. A mass suicide where we all joined hands and jumped off the Bosphorus Bridge. The famous strait proved narrow in the extreme. So narrow, in fact, that if the whole Istanbul experience was a suppository, it could find no escape once inside us. Every now and then, I feel it move, letting me know it's still there, asserting its presence. It calls me by name and it's a pain in the arse in the truest sense of the term.

When that torture of a game was finished, we sat like a bunch of half-wits in the dressing room there at the Atatürk Stadium. We were bloodthirsty zombies faced with an unforeseen problem – the blood was ours and they'd drunk every last drop. We couldn't speak. We couldn't move. They'd mentally destroyed us. The damage was already evident even in those early moments, and it only got more stark and serious as the hours went on. Insomnia, rage, depression, a sense of nothingness. We'd invented a new disease with multiple symptoms: Istanbul syndrome.

I no longer felt like a player, and that was devastating enough. But even worse, I no longer felt like a man. All of a sudden, football had become the least important thing, precisely because it was the most important: a very painful contradiction.

I didn't dare look in the mirror in case my reflection spat back at me. The only possible solution I could think of was to retire. And what a dishonourable retirement it would have been. My last performance had been so comically pathetic they wouldn't even have taken me on *Zelig*[32].

I glimpsed the end of the line: the journey was over. The story was finished and so was I. I walked with my head bowed even in the places I hold most dear. It wasn't to avoid sympathetic glances, just that when you don't know where you're going, looking ahead makes you tired and worried.

People talk about performance anxiety. Well, 'non-performance' anxiety is the perfect description for those of us who simply vanished from the pitch sometime during that final. The match in Istanbul was on May 25 and the Italian championship had yet to finish. We had to go back to Milanello to carry our cross for four more days, right up until Sunday, May 29, when we played our last Serie A match against Udinese. That parade of shame was the toughest punishment. A cavalcade of disgrace with us placed front and centre.

It was a brief, intense, shitty period. You couldn't escape or pull the plug on a world that had turned upside down, and you were forever surrounded by the other guilty parties in this theft of our own dignity. We always ended up talking about it. We asked each other questions, but nobody had any answers. We were a group of Gigi Marzullos[33] called to a collective psychoanalysis session with one fairly sizeable flaw: there wasn't any doctor, just a bunch of madmen. One thought he was Shevchenko, another Crespo, another Gattuso, Seedorf, Nesta, Kaká… I thought I was Pirlo. A gathering of impostors, too many to get away with it.

I could hardly sleep and even when I did drop off, I awoke to a grim thought: I'm disgusting. I can't play any more. I went to bed with Dudek and all his Liverpool teammates. The game against Udinese ended 0-0, goals a perfect stranger. A nightmare is a nightmare because you know it'll start when you close your eyes but won't stop when you reopen them, and so the torment went on.

We Milan players still had Italy commitments to (dis)honour, and it took Lippi only a few seconds to see precisely how things stood. "My boys, my boys, you're in bits." Congratulations on your intuition, Marcello. A blind man would have noticed – our devastation was legible even in braille. "Thanks for coming anyway," he said.

None of us could think straight. I greeted the staff at the training centre as if it was the last time I'd see them. In my head, that *was* the last time. Going off and doing something else with my life had to be better than feeling like this.

Painfully slowly, things started to improve during the holidays, even if the wounds didn't heal completely. The first day, I wanted to throw myself into a swimming pool with no water. The second day, there'd have been water, but I still wouldn't have wanted to re-emerge. The third day, I wanted to drown in the kids' pool. On the fourth, I'd have preferred to suffocate giving mouth to mouth to a rubber duck. I was getting better, but pretty much imperceptibly.

I'll never fully shake that sense of absolute impotence

when destiny is at work. The feeling will cling to my feet forever, trying to pull me down. Even now if I mess up a pass, that malign force could be to blame. For that reason, I steer well clear of the DVD from the Liverpool game. It's an enemy that I can't allow to wound me a second time. It's already done enough damage: most of it hidden far from the surface.

I'll never watch that match again. I've already played it once in person and many other times in my head, searching for an explanation that perhaps doesn't even exist. Praying for a different ending, like with those films you watch a second time hoping that you misunderstood the final scene. Surely the good guy can't die like that?

We rose again two years later, 2007, when we beat the self-same Liverpool in another Champions League final. We won in Athens thanks to an Inzaghi double – one of the goals was a free-kick from me that hit off him and went in[34].

The intensity of our joy was nothing compared to the deafening sound of our weaponry crashing to the ground a couple of years earlier. They say that revenge is a dish best served cold. Well, there was still a little warmth left in the corpse at that stage and, as such, we celebrated but didn't forget. We wanted to, but couldn't. The stain remained.

So much so that it was suggested we hang a black funeral pall as a permanent reminder on the walls of Milanello, right next to the images of triumph. A message to future generations that feeling invincible is the first step on the path to the point of no return.

Personally, I'd add that horrendous result to the club's honours board. I'd write it slap bang in the middle of the list of leagues and cups they've won, in a different coloured ink and perhaps a special font, just to underline its jarring presence. It would be embarrassing but, at the same time, it would enhance the worth of the successes alongside.

It's a trick that some housewives have perfected. They'll go to the supermarket and throw all sorts of big-brand goods into the trolley: San Daniele ham, Panna water, expensive parmesan cheese, Barolo wine. Then they'll chuck in a plain, sad little yoghurt that looks out of place beside the rest. When they get the shopping home, the husband and kids see the yoghurt. It's not what any of them would have picked, and they find the courage to pipe up. "Mamma, dearest, never buy that yoghurt again."

They see it for what it is: a huge mistake, a plunge in style, an exception that reinforces the rule. Thanks to that interloper in the trolley, the rest stands out. The housewife, with her shrewd intelligence, had it mapped out all along. A perfect plan to extol and encourage certain tastes by sacrificing another. Her family will never find that plain old yoghurt in the fridge again, just as I hope never to experience another night like May 25, 2005. I wouldn't be able to cope, even if I was a cat on my ninth and final life. I'd rather commit suicide by taking a stroll through a cage of ravenous Dobermans.

There are always lessons to be found in the darkest moments. It's a moral obligation to dig deep and find that little glimmer of hope or pearl of wisdom. You might hit upon an elegant phrase that stays with you and makes the journey that little less bitter. I've tried with Istanbul and haven't managed to get beyond these words: for fuck's sake.

31 Milan were 3-0 up at half-time through goals from Paolo Maldini and Hernan Crespo (2). Liverpool hit back after the break, Steven Gerrard, Vladimir Smicer and Xabi Alonso all getting on the scoresheet. There were no further goals in extra time. Liverpool won 3-2 on penalties

32 Woody Allen's mockumentary

33 Gigi Marzullo is a high-profile Italian talk-show host

34 Inzaghi's goals came right on the stroke of half-time and in the 82nd minute. Dirk Kuyt scored for Liverpool in the dying moments, but Milan held on to win 2-1

Chapter 13

That's right: for fuck's sake. Double fuck. The first words that come to my lips when I think of Istanbul. For me, it's now the capital of evil and forced cursing. Swearing's my release, and the one weapon I have to defend myself against destiny when it elects to strike without pity. I'm not superstitious, so I've got to have something to cling to.

Others go in for some real heavy stuff. People like Alberto Gilardino, my one-time team-mate with Milan and Italy, put their faith in witchcraft. Most of the items in his kitbag are real 'model footballer' territory: Dolce and Gabbana dressing gown, Dolce and Gabbana slippers, Dolce and Gabbana suit, Dolce and Gabbana briefs, Dolce and Gabbana glasses, Dolce and Gabbana cologne, and L'Oreal hair gel – only because Dolce and Gabbana don't make it.

But he'd always slip a pair of stinky old boots in there as well. We're talking ancient, ugly, tatty things with wobbly studs. Archaeological relics, if truth be told, but he treated them like treasure and they were always spotlessly clean. He'd shine them up, caress them; sometimes he'd even talk to them and kiss them. Mental stuff.

As they looked like something Attila the Hun might have played in, our kit supplier made him promise not to wear them in competitive games. They sat him down to explain that Sandro Pertini had long since stopped playing cards on planes[35], that you couldn't buy a black-and-white TV any more, and that John F Kennedy had been assassinated. This last piece of news in particular always seemed to take him aback ("are you serious?"), but he'd soon gather himself and his pride, saying: "I'm not chucking these boots away."

"But why, Gila? They've got more holes than a slice of Emmental."

"Because I've scored a shedload of goals in them. If I put them in the bag I take to the ground, they'll transmit the fluid to my new boots."

"The fluid?"

"The magic fluid."

"Oh Gila..."

"Honestly. And the more I put them in with my other kit, the better the chances that the magic fluid will come out the soles and spread to the new boots. Fingers crossed it'll work right away and have the desired effect."

"So first they need to be squeezed like lemons, then you sprinkle the juice on the other ones?"

"Spot on Andrea. Finally someone who understands. It doesn't take a genius."

"You're right about that – it doesn't take a genius..."

From what I know, the boots date back to when he played for Biellese[36] or thereabouts. Years later, just the sight of those wrecks with their frayed laces was enough to make him regress and lose his mind. They were his lucky charm –

without them he felt lost.

"If I've got them with me, I'll score goals. If I leave them at home by mistake, I'll ask the boss to stick me on the bench, because there's no way I'll do anything good without them."

Whatever you think of Gila's little quirk, it's considerably better than the more invasive ritual favoured by Filippo Inzaghi. Simply put, he crapped. Crapped a hell of a lot. That isn't a bad thing in itself, but the fact he'd do it at the ground, in our dressing room, just before the game, got on our nerves somewhat. Especially if the dressing room was small – a stink like that in such a confined space can get a little overpowering. Often he'd go three or four times in the space of 10 minutes.

"It brings me luck, boys," he'd say.

I'd heard that was the case if you stepped in it. That producing it and smelling it had the same effect was certainly news to me.

"It doesn't do much for us, Pippo," we'd say. "What have you been eating, anyway – a dead body?"

Inzaghi's answer was always the same. "Plasmons."

In hindsight, it was pointless even asking. We all knew those baby biscuits were what Pippo ate at all hours, every single day. He was a 40-year-old newborn. And when he came to the end of a pack, he had to leave two biscuits at the bottom. Not one, not three: two. "That way the stars will stay aligned in my favour." Ah yes, the famous alignment of the stars and baby biscuits.

"For goodness sake, don't touch the last couple. You'll just upset the balance," he'd say. The intestinal one, most likely.

We tried everything to steal the last two from him, but

never had any joy. He guarded them jealously, as selfish with his snacks as he was when it came to passing the ball. "I'm doing it for your own good, boys. You need my goals."

There was the same self-enforced monotony about the other things he ate. Plain pasta with a little bit of tomato sauce and cured beef for lunch. Plain pasta with a little bit of tomato sauce and cured beef for dinner. That was his lifelong menu. He behaved in the same way at the table as he did in the opposition penalty box. Always doing the same thing, without any great imagination or flair, but with maximum efficiency.

At meal times, he'd sit and wait for the waiter to bring the dishes, almost as if he wanted to be spoon-fed. During games, he'd sit and wait for the ball to somehow bounce off him and end up in the net.

And he'd always have on the same pair of boots. They were good for all seasons and he cherished them with a rather suspicious level of devotion. Over the years I've realised that all forwards are fetishists. Pippo's boots didn't have any magic fluid, but they did have loads of patches. Like Gilardino's, they dated back to the dawn of time, but there was a clear difference in the outlook of the respective owners.

"I'm well aware these boots are destroyed, but I'm going to keep playing in them," Pippo would say. "Nobody's ever going to change my mind. These are the only soft ones going."

"What are you on about?" we'd ask. "All boots that professional players use are soft."

"Nope, you're wrong. Only these ones are."

He was completely crazy but harmless. A really nice

fruitcake, if you like.

Sebastiano Rossi[37] wasn't much better (or worse, depending on how you look at it). He was a great big bear of a goalkeeper, over two metres tall and with a truly inexplicable obsession. When the team warmed up before a game, nobody could walk behind him. Under his strict house rules it was absolutely prohibited. "It's bad luck: you'd be as well sticking an own goal past me right now," he'd say.

Everyone at Milan knew about this quirk, but we weren't about to let on to our opponents. Guys like Angelo Peruzzi[38], his fellow keeper who happened to be playing at our ground one day. Now, at the San Siro there's a little gym where both teams warm up. Rossi was busy doing an exercise with our trainer and had his back glued to his favourite wall. It so happened that he dropped a ball and had to take a couple of steps forward to retrieve it. At that precise moment, he saw Peruzzi coming over. Walking quite calmly, headed straight for him.

Rossi instantly abandoned what he was doing and, to stop Peruzzi in his tracks, wedged himself between him and the wall. We all heard the commotion, followed by these words: "Get out of here, this is private property. Nobody walks behind me." It was as if he'd stuck up one of those signs you see with a picture of a dog with a line through it, replacing the face with that of Peruzzi.

There wasn't a scene purely because Peruzzi knew you don't attack crazy people. You smile, nod and agree.

"Seba, you could have hurt him," we said.

"Pity I didn't," came the reply.

In the dressing room, he'd commandeer all the scissors used to cut the tape that goes over your socks and shin guards. He absolutely had to be the first person to use them. Only after he'd finished were the rest of us allowed a shot.

"If we change this routine, we'll end up jinxed."

Whenever he said that, I followed the old custom of touching my balls, just in case for once in his life he was right.

Back in my Reggina days, the man to keep an eye on was Paolo Foglio[39]. He couldn't sleep unless he'd balanced his trainers against the wall, one on top of the other with the toes pointing down. A real feat of geometry.

It was funny to watch these guys tackling their various demons. To me, it seemed a complete waste of time. Superstitions tend to begin when something goes wrong. For a goalkeeper, it might be letting in too many goals. For a striker, a temporary inability to find the back of the net. For Inzaghi, a sudden strike at the Plasmon factory.

I manage to keep my head even in difficult times which, fortunately, have been few and far between. I reckon that people looking on from outside are pleased to see a pretty normal guy without too many excesses. I like it when I hear parents tell their kids: "Pirlo's got his head screwed on. Follow his example."

You can be a good player, a really good player, without going overboard on the pitch. You don't have to have a crazy haircut to be a point of reference for the team. I don't even really like tattoos, although I've actually got three small, well hidden ones: my son Niccolò's name in Chinese letters on my neck; an 'A' for his sister Angela just below, and my wife Debora's name on my ring finger, covered by my wedding band.

They're invisible to others: some sentiments should

belong to me alone. I feel them on my skin. I want them on my skin.

Compared to every other team I've played in, superstitious folks are thin on the ground at Juventus. Conte's very religious: before he goes onto the pitch, he'll kiss a crucifix and statuettes depicting saints, then move onto the Madonna and his rosary beads. I don't think he'd put up with some of the more tribal stuff.

Come to think of it, however, there's one exception to the rule: our president, Andrea Agnelli. During my first season at the club, he missed every single away game. "I feel sure of victory only when we're playing in Turin," he says. "Anywhere else, I pick up negative vibes."

To win the *scudetto*, we beat Cagliari at the Stadio Nereo Rocco in Trieste. The president wasn't there, but I'm saying nothing. The guy who pays my wages is always right.

35 Sandro Pertini was Italian president from 1978 to 1985. When Italy won the World Cup in 1982, he flew back from Spain with the team and was pictured playing cards with manager Enzo Bearzot as well as players Dino Zoff and Franco Causio. The World Cup itself was sat in the middle of the table

36 A club from the town of Biella in Piedmont, northwest Italy

37 Goalkeeper who started out with Cesena before spending over a decade at Milan

38 Goalkeeper who played for Roma, Juventus, Inter and Lazio, and was part of Italy's World Cup winning squad in 2006

39 A jobbing right-back who saw service with Reggina, Atalanta and Siena

Chapter 14

His uncle was known as the *avvocato*[40], his father was the *dottore*[41], and he's plain old Andrea. A simple title for a special man who's cut from the same cloth as all the other Agnelli. Lamb by name[42], lion by nature and never, ever caged. Always free to mingle with the common man.

Andrea is one of us, and one of them – he's a fan with special privileges because his words have the power to get the players on their feet and into action. The team belongs to him and to everyone: it's a communist co-operative at the heart of a capitalist state. He pays, the others celebrate, then he can rejoice as well.

Juventus isn't his plaything. It's something greater: a family passion, a private property that remains extremely public. A cause that he's inherited, cultivated, made bigger. He's a president, *the* president. Coming from the past to build the future. The present certainly exists as a crucial point on the *bianconero*[43] timeline, but somehow it's also fleeting.

The president's motto is "Work, work, and more work".

The reality is he doesn't need to but, for him, it's an insatiable desire. "The only way to win," he calls it. "The one path that will take you to your most ambitious goals."

His passion for Juventus is almost pathological. Friends of the club are always welcome, but its enemies must be stopped, as soon as humanly possible. He's not a nasty man by nature but if you're against him, you'll see that side. He always fights fire with fire: any perceived slight against Juventus is a slap in the face for him, and he'll react. He'll roar, grapple and hit out, with words that have the gravity of a sentence issued by a judge.

From the team's point of view, he's a very kind and caring president. He never raises his voice with us, however things are going. He'll be there by our side in sickness and in health until death do us part, because he's married to us and the club. His first thought is for us, and only then will he worry about himself. He loves us and we're all very aware of that fact.

Just like Conte, he knows what needs said and when, even if his tone is softer and less strident. He could talk about figures like Gianni and Umberto Agnelli[44] but never does. He could go on about Michel Platini, Roberto Baggio, maybe even Alessandro Del Piero, but they don't enter the conversation either.

He'll never go into detail about a particular dynasty or team from the club's past. He doesn't like making comparisons because it might cause embarrassment and that's just not his style. Many times, however, I've heard him say: "It's a privilege to play for Juventus. It's a beautiful thing, written into only a few people's destiny, and you should always thank your lucky stars that you're here. Everyone who's played for this club has won something sooner or later. One trophy, 10, a hundred. This club is everything, and it needs to be everything for you as well. You need to be Juventus to the very core of your being, always striving for further glory, for yourself and for the club. Take your lead from those who came before you. Be that inspiration for those who'll follow."

One brick and then another: happiness for him derives from a pretty straightforward plan.

Even when he's talking about something else, it always comes back to Juventus. The season after we won the title in Trieste[45], we were suffering a bit of a dip, and he started discussing the Ryder Cup in golf, another sport he adores. "Boys, there's this competition that takes place every two years where the strongest golfers in Europe and the United States play against each other. It's the absolute ultimate, the noblest thing they can be involved in. It's a real heaven on earth for these guys."

In 2012 it took place at Medinah Country Club, not far from Chicago.

"At the end of the first two days, the Americans were 10-6 up. They were on the verge of winning and making that ultimate dream a reality. They needed only four-and-a-half points and, for anyone who doesn't know, that's not really a lot. The Europeans, on the other hand, needed to win eight of the 12 singles matches to draw level and hold onto their trophy."

In essence, he was talking about people who wear caps with visors on their heads. Who go about with clubs in their hands and shiny shoes on their feet. Two groups of well-to-do gentlemen out for a stroll on perfect lawns. And yet he had us utterly captivated. He was pushing all the right buttons and we really got into the story. There was complete silence in that room, as if we were all holding our breath at the side of those greens in Illinois.

"During the last day of play, the Europeans pulled off a miracle. They didn't just draw; they won. Through sheer force of will. And will can take you everywhere, boys. It can tear down walls, give you wings and destroy differences. The Americans were absolutely powerless as they watched the greatest comeback in the history of the Ryder Cup taking shape before their eyes. They were swept away by that force, caught up in it against their will.

"The newspapers over there called it 'The Miracle of Medinah'. Boys, let's not give up. Let's give it everything we've got. Every last ounce within us."

Call me mad, but his words sent a shiver down my spine. Just for a moment, he reminded me of Al Pacino and his extraordinary performance in *Any Given Sunday*, the cult film where he plays an American football coach. Unforgettable words – cinema to make your heart race. I looked at our president and saw Pacino as he delivered his lesson in that husky voice. "Either we heal as a team, or we're gonna crumble. Inch by inch, play by play. Until we're finished. We're in hell right now, gentlemen. Believe me. And, we can stay here, get the shit kicked out of us, or we can fight our way back into the light. We can climb outta hell ... one inch at a time. But I can't do it for ya."

And so we did it for him. I went home that night, switched on the computer and began to research the Ryder Cup. I wanted to know more – Andrea had pricked my curiosity and got me all fired up. I learned the names of the main protagonists: José María Olazábal, the non-playing captain.

Rory McIlroy, Justin Rose, Paul Lawrie, Graeme McDowell, Francesco Molinari, Luke Donald, Lee Westwood, Sergio Garcia, Peter Hanson, Martin Kaymer, Nicolas Colsaerts, and Ian Poulter. Twelve names on the winning team, just like with Juventus. Our detractors reckon the twelfth man is the referee, but it's actually our fans. They're always at our side, at home and on the road. Them, us, Andrea: all for one. And Andrea for everyone.

The president and I hit it off straight away. We broke the ice the day I signed my contract in front of the camera crews and photographers at the Juventus HQ on Turin's Corso Galileo Ferraris.

"I'm pleased you're here, Andrea," he said.

"I'm here to win, Andrea," I replied.

"Hearing those words makes me happy."

Andrea made an excellent first impression on me, and I'd like to think the feeling is mutual. It was footballing love at first sight; something that was in no way guaranteed when you consider where I was arriving from.

As I've got to know him, I've realised we have another thing in common: as soon as he wins a trophy, he immediately wants to win another. He's never content to settle – he's quickly learned how you beat the big guns.

He's also given Juventus their old mentality back. It's one that really used to get on my wick as an opposition player. You always knew that they'd fight to the death and give every last drop of sweat. They'd never hold back: they'd get kicked and they'd get straight back up again. They'd score a goal and you just knew they'd get another one a few minutes later. You'd try to intimidate them and they'd just get angry. And when they were cross, they seemed to perform even better.

The whole *Calciopoli* thing lent a hand to the Juventus team of that time. But to my dying day, I'll remain convinced they would have won the same number of trophies relying on their own means, without any kind of external assistance.

And that's why I wore a t-shirt with the slogan '30 [titles] won on the pitch' after we clinched the league in Trieste. I came from a world that went to war with Juventus over what happened but, for me, a title that's taken away and then not assigned or handed to another team remains an honour you've won. If you're not a *bianconero*, or if you don't become one as I did, you'll never understand. Winning that title was a return to normality, a soft landing delayed for several years by turbulence.

It's certainly helped that Andrea's a combative president, but also someone with no airs or graces who lives his life like any other man his age[46]. He's happy to stroll about Turin in his jeans and stop to talk to anyone. He answers supporters' questions, takes their advice on board, listens to their criticisms. He'll explain where he's coming from and doesn't hide away. He lives and breathes the city and understands what people are thinking. I'd love to see him become mayor one day.

After the first *scudetto* won on his watch, he came to celebrate with us at the Cacao club in the city's Parco del Valentino. He really let his hair down, dancing, drinking and even having a go on the karaoke. I can't remember whether the song he picked was *Fuck You* by Marco Masini (even though he's a Fiorentina fan) but I'd really like to think so. A special dedication to those who'd refused to believe.

To us players, he said thanks. "You're my pride and joy. I've been president only for a short while, and you've given

me an extraordinary gift. I knew we'd become the best in Italy, but I thought it would take us longer. Ah, but Italy's not enough for me any more!"

In my head, I could hear the Champions League theme tune. Andrea winked at me. Andrea Agnelli: 100 per cent Agnelli[47].

40 The lawyer

41 The doctor

42 The Italian for lamb is *agnello*, plural *agnelli*

43 Juventus's nickname: literally the 'white and blacks'

44 Famous past presidents at Juventus, cornerstones of the Agnelli dynasty. Gianni is Andrea's uncle and Umberto his father

45 Season 2012-13

46 Andrea Agnelli was born in 1975

47 A label endorsing quality as you might find on a food packet or item of clothing: 100% Agnello (100% lamb/lambswool)

Chapter 15

Andrea had me in his sights after we won that first title. He took aim and fired, but it was flowers, not bullets that came flying out. Make love not war, he seemed to be saying. And if you've time left over, grab yourself a goal and dedicate it to me.

He appeared almost disbelieving as he lived out that dream in all its wonderful lightness. He was absolutely made up: in the seventh heaven of happiness. There were no clouds around, just 30 sunbeams shining on the pitch, one for each title. They say you shouldn't stare at the sun, but Andrea seemed set on burning his retinas. When it's paradise you're beholding, you've no need to wear sunglasses. If anything, they spoil a smiling face, making it seem dull and coarse.

If we're talking longing looks, however, nothing compares to the ones I got from André Schembri one ordinary night in Modena. I'm convinced the Malta midfielder had fallen for me: I could almost see the love hearts dancing about his face. He had his eyes glued on me from the very first minute of the match. Those eyes became fully his again only when we were back in our respective dressing rooms.

That game was in 2012, more precisely September 11 of that year. Schembri was like some kind of footballing kamikaze. Or perhaps just a kamikaze of love. He certainly had no interest in the ball – he treated it as if it was burst and thus completely without purpose. The only thing that counted was my presence at his side, or, more accurately, his presence at mine. We rolled along together, me and my imperfect shadow. I'd move, and he'd follow. I'd slow down, and he'd pull up the handbrake, too. I was the victim of a close encounter of the third kind. Had we been alone in a dark alley and not on a football pitch in front of 20,000 fans, I'd have called the cops. I'd have been within my rights to report that his passion had turned a little violent, because he certainly wasn't holding back on the physical stuff.

"What the fuck are you doing?" I asked him.

"Sorry?" came the reply.

"What are you up to? You've been staring at me so long you must know every inch of my face. You're booting me up and down the pitch and you've not even touched the ball yet. Do you maybe want to think about actually playing and not just trotting around after me?"

"Not possible. Our coach said the only thing I should think about is marking you. That and nothing else. My mission is to stop you."

"Yes, but the ball's away over there. It's miles from us. At least let me breathe – you don't need to be 10 centimetres from my face the whole time."

"Who gives a toss about the ball? I've to watch you. You and nothing else."

Had he been in possession of a ring, I'm sure he'd have

got down on one knee and proposed. "I, André, take you, Andrea, as my lawful wedded target. To kick you, follow you and chop you all the days of my life, until ref do us part."

The way he was carrying on really got on my nerves. I'd love to think that leeches are an endangered species, not one that's perpetually on heat. But every time I end up disappointed. Malta were playing Italy, but Schembri was playing only me. An experience like that is enough to drive you mad. It's just utterly exhausting.

"Are you actually having fun out here? I feel sorry for you," I said.

"Who said anything about having fun? I'm simply carrying out the coach's orders."

"But you're never going to enjoy the game like this."

"Ah, but neither are you."

And he was absolutely right. I didn't enjoy it, and it wasn't the first or last time. Back in the day, coaches would have their best guy mark the opposition No.10. He was the player who tended to have the most class and so the objective was obvious: stop him touching the ball.

Things have changed since then, though. Football has moved on, and it's now the centre midfielders who get the most attention. Guys in my position are the ones who plot and construct the play and it's us who now have the toughest bloke on the other team snapping away at our heels.

It's always the same – every game I'll leave the pitch with a load of bruises. I've even had Francesco Totti taking aim at me in a match we played against Roma[48]. Every so often he does go off on one, but at least he apologised afterwards. The foul he committed really wasn't like him and I'm sure he didn't do it deliberately. I certainly don't have any issue with him now.

It's not easy to tame a mastiff that's running around after you for a full 90 minutes. He's the dog and you're the bone: that's just how it is for me, even if I'll never get used to it. Football's becoming more and more like wrestling and that's really not a good thing.

I usually wind up swapping shirts with my pursuer at the end of a game. I even went through the ritual with Schembri. When you've been studied so intently for an hour-and-a-half, it's as if you've known each other your whole lives. I always try to give these guys the slip. I'll look to get into space and find a way to take the ball and play my normal game; to do my thing even with chains around my ankles. But there are times when it's bloody hard. Even players who don't have much ability can run and tackle all day long. They might be brainless robots, but they'll have the physique of the craziest gym monkey. If I manage to dribble past them, they'll never catch me in a million years. But if I run into them, it'll hurt.

Opposition managers must be scared of me, otherwise they'd never employ these tactics, but knowing that is scant consolation. Pretty much all the guys who tail me aren't really bothered about the constructive side of the game. They'll join in with an attack if they have to but as soon as they've lost the ball they'll be back at my side, forgetting about everything else. They just want to knock me down.

Even Sir Alex Ferguson, the purple-nosed manager who turned Manchester United into a fearsome battleship, couldn't resist the temptation. He's essentially a man without blemish, but he ruined that purity just for a moment when it came to me. A fleeting shabbiness came over the legend that night.

On one of the many occasions where our paths crossed during my time at Milan, he unleashed Park Ji-Sung to shadow me. The midfielder must have been the first nuclear-powered South Korean in history, in the sense that he rushed about the pitch at the speed of an electron. Back and forth he went. He'd try to contribute in attack and if that didn't work, he'd fling himself at me. He'd have his hands all over my back, making his presence felt and trying to intimidate me. He'd look at the ball and not know what it was for. An unidentified rotating object, to his eyes. They'd programmed him to stop me and that was the only thing he was thinking about. His devotion to the task was almost touching. Even though he was already a famous player in his own right, he consented to being used as a guard dog, willingly limiting his own potential.

I live every one of these experiences as a gross injustice, and it's not uncommon for me to feel real pity for whoever's sent to watch me. They're players – more than that, they're men – who've been asked to go out there and act without dignity, destroying instead of creating. They're happy to come across as utter crap as long as they make me look bad, too.

I'm a bit of a wandering gypsy on the pitch. A midfielder continually on the lookout for an unspoilt corner where I can move freely just for a moment, without suffocating markers or randy Maltese guys sticking to me like shadows. All I'm after is a few square metres to be myself. A space where I can continue to profess my creed: take the ball, give it to a team-mate, team-mate scores. It's called an assist and it's my way of spreading happiness.

It's probably this movement from one area of the field

to another (albeit on foot rather than by caravan) that gave rise to the story that I come from a Roma family. Or, to be more accurate, a Sinti[49] one. The rumour first appeared in a high-profile newspaper article just before the Italy v Romania game at Euro 2008. At first I let it go, simply smiling at the headlines, but before long the media onslaught became unbearable. Some really serious untruths were said and written about my family, and they started spying on everything we did. They wrote stories about our daily habits, the places we went, the people we met. It was an annoying and dangerous invasion of our privacy and that of those we hold dear.

I've a pretty good idea as to how the rumour came about. As well as producing wine, my father Luigi has links with the steel trade. He and my brother are both involved with a company called Elg Steel. The metal trade has traditionally been the most popular line of work with the Sinti and, as such, somebody must have put two and two together to come up with five. The green light for a series of utterly crazy articles.

If I'd issued a strongly worded correction, a categorical denial, I'd have run the risk of causing offence. It would have looked like I was trying to distance myself from the Sinti community and position myself against them. My desire to state the truth could have been wrongly interpreted as an act of racism, and that's a risk I wasn't willing to take, for the simple reason that I find racists disgusting.

I'm not a Sinti, but saying that publically could have sparked a whole chain of mishaps, more for them than for me. At that point, it would have been their privacy being invaded and destroyed. There would have been a race to shine a light on the world that Andrea Pirlo had talked about. I know the pitfalls of certain situations with the media and, in this instance, I chose to avoid them.

The people who belong to that ethnic group are simply part of another culture. They're made in one way, and we're made in another. Two stories that are equally beautiful; two pieces of the same jigsaw.

I didn't put things straight then so I'll go ahead and do it now, saying what I would have liked to have done right at the start. My family have always hailed from Lombardy. I'm from Brescia, I'm Italian, I'm not a Sinti. And, most of all, I've got nothing against the Sinti. If I did, there would be something seriously wrong.

---

48 During a Roma v Juventus game in 2013, a foul by Francesco Totti caused Pirlo to leave the field for some time. Totti was booked and went on to score the only goal in the game

49 The Sinti are a Romani people from central Europe

Chapter 16

I'm Italian, but I'm also part-Brazilian. Pirlinho, if you like. When I take my free-kicks, I think in Portuguese and at most I'll do the celebrating in my native tongue.

I strike those dead balls *alla Pirlo*. Each shot bears my name and they're all my children. They look like one another without being twins, even if they do boast the same South American roots. More precisely, they share a source of inspiration: Antonio Augusto Ribeiro Reis Junior, a midfielder who's gone down in history as Juninho Pernambucano[50].

During his time at Lyon, that man made the ball do some quite extraordinary things. He'd lay it on the ground, twist his body into a few strange shapes, take his run-up and score. He never got it wrong. Never. I checked out his stats and realised it couldn't just be chance. He was like an orchestra conductor who'd been assembled upside down, with the baton held by his feet instead of his hands. He'd give you the thumbs up by raising his big toe – somebody at Ikea was having a good laugh the day they put him together.

I studied him intently, collecting DVDs, even old photographs of games he'd played. And eventually I understood. It wasn't an immediate discovery; it took patience and perseverance. From the start, I could tell he struck the ball in an unusual way. I could see the 'what' but not the 'how'. And so I went out onto the training pitch and tried to copy him, initially without much success. In the early days, the ball sailed a couple of metres over the crossbar, or three metres above the sky to borrow from the Italian film of the same name.

Much of the time it went right over the fence at Milanello and I'd end up lying to the fans gathered outside, pretending I'd done it deliberately. "Boys, I want to give you a present," I'd say, glossing over the fact that the session was behind closed doors and they shouldn't have been anywhere near it. As I was speaking to outlaws, I told myself that what I said was neither a sin nor a crime.

The misses went on for several days and by that time the bloke in charge of the kit store was getting somewhat peeved. For him, it was a case of too many lost balls becoming a ball ache as I persisted with my experiments. Days soon turned into weeks.

The best ideas come about in moments of total concentration, a state you can reach when shitting, as Filippo Inzaghi will attest. My own Eureka moment arrived when I was sat on the toilet. Hardly romantic, but there you go. The search for Juninho's secret had become an obsession for me, to the extent that it occupied my every waking thought. It was at the point of maximum exertion that the dam burst, in every sense of the term. The magic formula was all about *how* the ball was struck, not *where*: only three of Juninho's toes came into contact with the leather, not his whole foot as you might expect.

The next day I left the house really early, even electing to skip the classic PlayStation battle with Nesta as I rushed to the training paddock. All I had on my feet was a pair of loafers – I didn't need proper boots to demonstrate what I was now convinced was the right theory.

The kit-store guy had already turned up for duty.

"Can you pass me a ball, please?" I asked.

"Get to fuck," he said under his breath, almost hissing at me.

"What was that?" I replied.

"I said I saw a duck."

"Right you are. Go on, you fool, throw me over a ball."

Reluctantly, he chucked one across. Mentally, he was already preparing himself for a trip to the woods to recover it. Instead I stuck it right in the top corner, just where the post meets the crossbar. A geometric gem. I placed the shot so perfectly that it would have gone in even with a keeper. Luckily for our goalies, none of them were around.

"Why don't you try doing that again, Andrea," came a provocative voice from behind. This was now a battle of two against one. Me on one side, the kit-store guy and the ghost of Juninho Pernambucano firmly on the other.

"Okay then, spoilsport. Just you watch," I said.

Up I stepped and unleashed a carbon copy of the previous free-kick. It was a thing of absolute beauty, stylistically impeccable. I lined up another five strikes and it was the same story every time. By now it was official: I'd cracked it. The secret was no more.

In essence, the ball needs to be struck from underneath

using your first three toes. You have to keep your foot as straight as possible and then relax it in one fell swoop. That way, the ball doesn't spin in the air, but does drop rapidly towards the goal. That's when it starts to rotate. And that, in a nutshell, is my *maledetta*[51].

When it comes off exactly as I want, there's no way of keeping it out. It's specifically designed to head over the wall before taking a direction that nobody can predict. For me, the best feeling in life is watching the ball fly into the net after it whizzes a couple of centimetres over the heads of the defenders. They can almost reach it, but not quite. They can read the maker's name, but they can't stop it going in. Sometimes a pinch of sadism is the ingredient that makes victory taste that little bit sweeter.

The further away from goal I am, the better. As the distance increases, so does the effect I can impart. The greater the space between me and the keeper, the quicker the ball tends to drop as it hones in on its target.

I can obviously mix things up a bit, throw in a few little tricks to make every free-kick unique, but the underlying concept never changes. Scoring from a dead-ball brings me massive satisfaction. It sets me up as an example for other players to follow, copy and perhaps even emulate over the course of time. For them, I'm a Juninho Pernambucano 2.0, a Brazilian with a Brescia accent.

I've never told anyone, but my ambition is to become the leading all-time scorer of free-kicks in Serie A. It's a goal that I've been working towards for several years now. When I was a kid, I'd stick a sofa in front of our living-room window and use it as a wall for shooting practice with a sponge ball. Nine times out of 10, the ball would fly over the sofa and end up between the glass and the actual wall: right where I'd aimed it.

Back in those days, I'd buy the Gazzetta dello Sport just to get my hands on the videos they sold with the paper showing the best free-kicks from the great No.10s. I'd press play and Baggio, Zico and Platini would spring into action. Great invention, the remote control – one push of a button and your imagination runs wild.

I can't abide the cliché "only the team's success matters – I don't care about my own". It's the tiresome complaint of those who have no personal ambition, whether for want of class or lack of character. For me, the team counts a huge amount but if I forgot about myself, I'd be doing my team-mates a disservice. Many individuals make a team, just as many dreams make a triumph. And if you're really lucky, they make history as well.

Although free-kicks are my passion, I've never had, or asked for, a bonus relating to the number I score. That would be a step too far. Easy money, in all probability, but not a road I've ever wanted to go down. Even if I did have a clause written into my contract, it's not something I'd obsess about, unlike a lot of strikers with their goals. All of them have bonuses triggered when they reach a certain number and it can make them very selfish. That's in their nature anyway, but having those huge extra sums dangled in front of them only serves to amplify the trait. I suppose it would be weird if it had the opposite effect. I can put up with strikers even if they're a bit capricious. Often I downright adore them.

One part of my job I'll never learn to love is the pre-match warm-up. I hate it with every fibre of my being. It actually disgusts me. It's nothing but masturbation for conditioning coaches, their way of enjoying themselves at the players' expense.

I've no doubt it helps you avoid injury, but it's still the worst part of our working week: a 15-minute pain in the arse. Quarter of an hour completely wasted. Most of the time I'll be thinking about something else as I go through the motions. I end up pretty much walking: my way of protesting against that unbearable procession. It's even worse if you're playing on the road, because then you've got to listen to the insults of the home fans.

I've absolutely no interest in jogging to warm up my muscles. The muscle that counts the most is the heart, and mine's always set at 100 degrees, burning with positive energy. I've explained my outlook to the various coaches I've worked with but none of them pays any attention. They'll look at me like I've just arrived from Mars, particularly when I suggest we also get rid of the warm-up before training.

If it was up to me, I'd have us playing straight away, during the week as well as on our Saturday and Sunday match-days. In the league, the Coppa Italia, the Champions League, whatever. Even the World Cup, which I managed to win despite doing no more than walk about during the 900 seconds that preceded the games against Ghana, USA, Czech Republic, Australia, Ukraine, Germany and France.

I hate the warm-up so much I need to do something to avoid getting depressed. And so I'll run a mental countdown, continually reminding myself that I must stay calm; that in a few minutes, the torture will be over.

Maybe it's a phobia. But the way I see it, I'm simply reacting to an injustice being inflicted on beauty. If you've

got Bar Refaeli[52] lying naked in front of you, you can't just wink at her and say: "Wait there, I'll be with you in 15 minutes." All you'll do in that quarter of an hour is think of her. You'll hold everything back until you've got her in your arms and can throw yourself into the moment.

It's exactly the same when you're about to play Real Madrid, Barcelona or any other superpower. All you want to do is get stuck into them, without any waiting around. You can't take your eyes off them and you begin to drool. You get wound up, think about what you're doing and then you get downright angry. Because you realise you're just wasting time.

---

50 A master of the dead ball, Juninho Pernambucano excelled with Lyon domestically and in the Champions League and won 40 caps for Brazil

51 Maledetta literally means 'cursed' or 'damned', mirroring how the opposition goalkeeper tends to feel

52 An Israeli model who has fronted campaigns for leading global brands

Chapter 17

Alessandro Del Piero gets where I'm coming from. It's only on his face that I've seen the same sort of look that disfigures mine during the pre-match warm-up. His last year at Juventus sticks in my mind as a kind of sporting agony; the drawn out death of an intense love that's destined to disappear, second by second, piece by piece, until it's nothing but one-way affection. And if there's only fondness on one side, the whole thing becomes a bit pointless.

He wasn't playing and he was suffering as a result. It was eating him up inside, and that unhappiness was obvious on the exterior. He looked like he wanted to smash up the world and everything in it: his face said it all about the horror he was living.

He tried to disguise his true feelings, but couldn't quite pull it off. In this life, you're either a man or an actor, there's nothing in between. Alessandro's attempt to put on a brave face proved pretty terrible and, as such, the example he set was priceless. He's a one-off and the same guy now he's always been. The fact that Sydney's a 24-hour flight from

Turin hasn't changed him one bit. He's a champion at home and abroad.

He suffered like crazy sitting on the bench that final year. Not letting him near a ball was the worst kind of punishment for him. He had a full season of being sent to bed with no dinner and no No.10. All he got was a pair of black-and-white striped pyjamas without a name on the back. The classic garb of a prisoner who hasn't been put to death but is condemned to permanent exile.

Never once did Alessandro complain in front of his team-mates; he always showed great dignity. You wouldn't see much of him in the dressing room during the week – he had his own personal trainer to put him through his paces because, after all, the perfect engine deserves special care and attention. In the mornings, he'd always arrive before everyone else, get changed and hole himself up in a little gym a few metres along from the one used by the rest of the squad. He'd join the main group only when the balls appeared and it was time to work on the technical stuff. When we needed him, he was there, and we were very aware of his presence. We were all pretty sad that a true champion like him had to leave, particularly when the team (*his* team) had just started winning again.

Even though we knew how the story would end, it was still upsetting. After all, we're talking about one of the most historic standard bearers in Juventus history. And when I say historic, I'm talking about his influence as well as his age.

I don't know exactly what went on between him and president Agnelli. I couldn't tell you which internal mechanism stopped working or what little bug got into the system – I've never thought it appropriate to ask. I've got

huge respect for both men, and there must be a valid reason for them having reached the end of the line. It's purely their business, a private matter that all started with differing views on a contract extension that never actually materialised.

It's a shame really, because Del Piero still had plenty to offer Juventus. A guy like him is always going to come in handy. Great people and exemplary professionals are the sort of folks I'd want at my side 24 hours a day and Alessandro is both those things.

It's not by chance that he's had such a world-class career. Even in those latter days, he'd still put on a masterclass of nobility whenever he got some game-time. The very essence of beauty presented in summary form: a few pages, a brief look, and you'd learned the lesson. Those moments were his chance to become a child again, even if he wasn't far away from hitting 40. More than once, he cried in front of everyone, holding nothing back. Just as a kid would, in fact.

After his penultimate appearance in a Juventus jersey (a home game against Atalanta in May 2012), he was finally overwhelmed by all the emotions he'd managed to keep a lid on up till then. His ego, his desire to be involved, that need to feel like a true *bianconero*. He flooded the dressing room with tears, and we did the same, both with him and for him. And then we said goodbye before he headed off to Sydney.

Alessandro chose the other side of the world to start over and carry on his career. It couldn't have gone any other way, really. If he'd stayed in Italy or moved to another league close by, he'd have just ended up feeling terribly homesick. Juventus is an almost physical attraction for him: it's like putting one magnet next to another.

Thanks to my pathological devotion to the Italy jersey, people say I'm a player who belongs to everyone. Sometimes I'll find opposition fans applauding me when we play on the road. Del Piero went one step further: supporters of other teams put him on a pedestal because he was a one-club man. They loved his dedication; the fact that he'd married a cause and stayed faithful, becoming something more than a mere footballer, as well as one of the all-time greats.

Earning that sort of reaction is nothing short of miraculous in an age when Juventus have started winning again and are thus widely disliked. The problem is that, all too often, sporting rivalry descends into the most boorish kind of hate. Pure ignorance throws open the doors to some quite barbaric behaviour.

In other countries, when the team buses arrive it's a truly joyous spectacle. You walk into the ground with a throng of fans on either side; the kids are all happy and so are we. Only very rarely do we need blacked-out windows to travel to the stadium.

In Italy, by contrast, away games are a nightmare. The journey between the team hotel and the ground is like an assault course. I'm sick of needing a police escort, of having cop cars in front and behind with their lights flashing and sirens blaring. The police should be dealing with more important things than worrying about us. Anti-mafia judges deserve to have guardian angels protecting them; we footballers can do without. In an ideal world, that is, but sadly not in Serie A.

We're way behind, and we don't seem to realise that the further we fall, the deeper and narrower the well has become. Smoke bombs, tear gas, sticks, rocks, bolts, plates... we've had everything thrown at us in our time. There was a game away to Napoli during my second season at Juventus when I thought things were going to end really badly. I've rarely been engulfed by a hell on earth quite like it. Hundreds of people came to wait for us outside our hotel and started throwing insults as soon as we tried to board the bus. I can live with that and I can just about live with them chucking eggs as well, but the situation deteriorated quickly.

As we got closer to the San Paolo, more and more objects rained down on us. We'd become the bullseye in a perverse game of Hit the *Juventino*. A few guys took refuge on the floor of the bus, particularly after a brick struck the window where Kwadwo Asamoah was sitting. Thankfully, the glass broke out the way, otherwise we could have been looking at a real tragedy. A surreal silence reigned in the bus thereafter. We'd realised that we weren't travelling for free. The risk of paying for my ticket with my life does trouble me from time to time at night when I'm trying to get to sleep.

Who can guarantee that one day, instead of a brick, someone's not going to pull out a gun? How do you control hundreds of people at the side of road, whose sole objective is to harm us? Who is willing to bet against there being one madman who is just that little bit nastier that the rest?

Whenever Juventus play away, bodyguards travel with us. Special agents are also a fixed presence, but is that always going to be enough? It's a terrible thing to contemplate, but I'd be lying if I said I never have. In any event, it's right to talk about it. People need to know about this rotten stuff on the outer edges of our world. And it's the same story in the north of Italy as it is in the centre or the south. Anyone who tries to make a geographical distinction is getting it badly wrong.

During the games themselves, Juventus are viewed like a bunch of Beagle Boys[53], robbers with stolen goods secreted about our persons. They call us thieves, an accusation with roots in the past. But if we're talking about days gone by, let's mention Serie B. A very recent, and very painful atonement that many people outside the club pretend to have forgotten. Too convenient, guys.

This business of singing songs against the other team is a very Italian speciality. The first commandment is 'insult thy opposition' and, if there's time left over, by all means encourage your own team. Leaving aside the grounds where people remember I play for Italy, I'm a piece of shit or a son of a whore. If I get booted by one of their team, they tell me I need to die.

Let's be honest about this: we're not far away from the abyss. The risk of violence is ever greater. It won't take much for us to topple over the edge, without even realising it's happening.

The *ultras* consider just about every ground in Italy a place where anything goes. A place where they can do and say whatever comes into their head. If I stop someone on the street and call them a wanker, at the very least they'll report me. But in the stands thousands of people do it all at the same time and nothing ever happens.

We lack that sporting culture you tend to see elsewhere. We can work on that, slowly, and we players can do our bit by not going overboard with what we say. But there's also an obvious lack of legal powers and, above all, a shortage of grounds that are actually owned by the clubs who play there.

Juventus Stadium is an absolute diamond in this regard – it's worth at least 10 points a year to us, thanks to the

positive atmosphere it helps create. The authorities know the name of the fan sitting in every seat and there are stewards and CCTV as well. In an environment like that, if you do something you shouldn't, it'll be spotted in real time. They see you, and then they come to find you.

Ideally, you'd want people to behave because it's the right thing to do but in certain cases it's fine if they only do it because they're afraid of ending up in the eye of the storm. It's a start, if nothing else.

If I was a politician (and thank the Lord I'm not), I'd fight to have cells built into the stadiums. Mini prisons like you find at the English grounds. If someone's acting up, stick them inside; don't give them a good kicking then immediately release them. And once you've got them in the cell, throw open the windows. God knows we need some fresh air.

53 The Beagle Boys were a gang of villainous dogs Scrooge McDuck in the Disney cartoon

Chapter 18

We also need Mario Balotelli. I'm not sure he really appreciates it yet, but he's a special kind of medicine, an antidote to the potentially lethal poison of the racists you find in Italian grounds.

They're a truly horrendous bunch, a herd of frustrated individuals who've taken the worst of history and made it their own. And they're more than just a minority, despite what certain mealy-mouthed spin doctors would have you believe. Those guys would use a fire extinguisher to put out a match.

Whenever I see Mario at an Italy training camp, I'll give him a big smile. It's my way of letting him know that I'm right behind him and that he mustn't give up. A gesture that means 'thank you'.

He's often targeted and insulted by opposition fans. Let's say that the way he goes about his business perhaps doesn't help him get much love, but I'm still convinced that if he was white, people would leave him in peace.

'Jump up high so Balotelli dies' is an unspeakable chant

that, sadly, I've heard at the Juventus Stadium amongst other places. Even worse are the monkey noises that I've listened to pretty much everywhere.

But instead of depressing Mario, moronic behaviour of that kind actually seems to fire him up. He won't let this human trash get their way, and it's the most intelligent response because if you listen to what a stupid person says, you elevate them to the position of interlocutor. If you simply ignore them (still acknowledging that, unfortunately, they exist) you're leaving them to stew in their own polluted sea: one where there are no friends and no shore. The good news is that even sharks can die of loneliness after a while.

Prandelli has given us national team players some firm direction on the matter. "If you hear people in the stands disrespecting Mario, run over to him and hug him." In that way, hate can be cancelled out by an equivalent dose of love. Not a fashionable choice, but a pretty forceful idea.

Speaking in purely theoretical terms, I wouldn't be willing to walk off the pitch in protest like Kevin-Prince Boateng did during a friendly against Pro Patria, taking the rest of the Milan team with him[54]. I don't think it's the best way to make a stand again racism: for me, it's more a surrender than a reaction.

That said, if one of my team-mates was a victim of intolerance and refused to carry on playing, I'd go along with his wishes and those of the rest of the team. It would be up to him to tell us how he felt and to take the final decision. I'd leave the field only if the whole team was in agreement, though. I think you'd have to actually experience something like that to know how you'd react. It's too delicate a subject to plan your response in advance.

I'm happy that Mario is the way he is. He'll react (wrongly) to provocation on the pitch, but doesn't let what's going on in the crowd affect him. If he scores, he might put his finger to his lips to mock the opposition fans, something that really infuriates them, but if they tell him he's got the wrong colour of skin he'll simply laugh in their faces. He makes complete fools of them and emerges a convincing winner. The way I see it, he's capable of becoming a symbol of the fight against racism, both in Italy and throughout the world.

In terms of footballing ability, Mario's class is unquestionable. I'd have happily seen him end up in a Juventus shirt. Top players are in a position of real strength, in that they can basically pick their club. The problem for us, however, is that there's only ever been one team in Mario's head. "Boys, sooner or later I'll sign for Milan," is the refrain we've all heard, and his dream duly became reality. I'd have loved to set up a few goals for him, playing a part in his success as I do with the national team. Only once did I think it might happen, when he said in an interview with Sky: "I'd really like to change the Juve fans' minds about me."

Maybe one day in the future we'll play in the same club side. I say that knowing that his agent, Mino Raiola, an absolutely world-class operator, would sell his own name to close a deal. And I mean that quite literally. He once admitted as much speaking to the co-author of this book.

"Mino, clear something up for me. How do you pronounce your surname? Is it *Rai*ola or Rai*ola*?

"Whatever you want, just as long as you pay me."

Give that man a round of applause.

For Mario, Juventus would have been a hyperbaric chamber. Somewhere he could let it all out and keep the pressure around him at a constant, ideal level. Buffon, Chiellini, Marchisio: when you look at those guys you realise just where you are. They're always happy, always ready to involve and excite you with their infectious enthusiasm. And, when required, they can also make you change your mind.

Balotelli would have been loved and nurtured by a dressing room where hard work is the order of the day. Where the spirit of sacrifice is an absolute must, not a request where you can shake your head and say 'no'.

Nobody ever moans and there are a load of Italy players about the place – perhaps the most precious strength of that whole environment. They're all steeped in the history of the club and know by heart the peaks and troughs it has experienced. They don't need any hints or clues as to who the good guys are and whose name needs a little cross. The national team players pull everyone along – they're our happy driving force.

It was the same at Milan, but it wasn't like that at Inter. Prandelli knows how it works at Juventus, and he usually calls us up to his squad *en bloc*. There's no one single person in command. The whole thing works so well because of the democratic spirit that reigns in the dressing room. If Buffon really wanted to, he could quite easily stand up and say: "I'll decide what happens here. I'm the captain; I've played in Serie B with this shirt on." But he's never done that and never will. He's too intelligent, too good, too everything really.

Lots of fans will go crazy when they read this, but I'm convinced our recent success has come about precisely because we were demoted. It helped amplify to the nth degree the sense of belonging at the club, which emerged from the whole thing strengthened. Getting back to Serie A was hard but, over the years, that pure anger has been transformed into something more positive. Now there's no more room for shame: being a *Juventino* is to carry oneself with pride and dignity. Till the very end, as president Agnelli would say.

When the negative vibes were cleansed, the resulting explosion brought about something remarkable. It was a black-and-white Big Bang, the creation of a new world very similar to the old one. And that's the really good news: Juventus descends from itself.

People are scared of us again, and it's getting more and more that way. We're reminded of that fact every day by numerous individuals, chief amongst them one Antonio Conte, when he sticks up on the dressing-room door the articles where opponents talk about us. He collects and cuts out these interviews with an almost maniacal zeal, attaching them to the entrance to that most secret room.

He takes a red highlighter to the bits he really wants us to read. People talk about the labourer president[55]; well, we've got the newsagent manager. At least once a week there's a summary session of what's been said in the papers. The message is clear. When it's Juventus they're playing, everyone takes on a completely different character, even those without hope at the bottom of the league with nothing left to play for. They'll try to claim a big scalp by getting under our skin. It's all about provocation.

"Boys, have you seen what this guy's saying?" Conte will ask. "He reckons we've got weak spots."

"It's all bullshit, coach," we'll say.

"It might be bullshit, but if we're men, we need to stand

up and show him he's wrong. And look at this guy. He swears we're going to go through a bad patch soon."

"That's a load of crap as well, coach."

"Let's not fall into this trap. There's only one way to prove him wrong and that's to win. Which reminds me – have you read this last line, the one I've circled?"

"Yes coach. That cretin says we're the most unlovable team in the world and that everybody knows it."

"He's right about that. When we see him out on the pitch, we need to thank him for saying it. It's a compliment: it means that we're back. That people are scared of us, that we're honouring the name we carry. Always remember this: opposition teams only really like those they know aren't going to beat them."

"Coach, he also says you're crazy."

"Do you see? In amongst the thousands of idiotic things he said, he's had a moment of clarity. Now, you owe me one euro twenty."

"What for?"

"The paper."

---

54 A friendly match between Milan and lower-league club Pro Patria in January 2013 was abandoned after players walked off in protest at racist chanting from fans. The game, played in Busto Arsizio near Milan, saw Pro Patria supporters single out Kevin-Prince Boateng and other black Milan players for abuse. Boateng tore off his shirt and walked off the pitch, and the rest of his teammates followed him

55 Silvio Berlusconi is known as the *presidente operaio*, a reference to his pride in being a self-made man

Chapter 19

Matri's paying. Matri[56] always pays, in a figurative sense as much as anything. Nesta's emigrated to Canada, I only see De Rossi when we're with the national team, and so Alessandro's the last man standing. It's an unwritten rule that my current roomie is always my first victim.

To be honest, sometimes it's like shooting at the Red Cross, even if he'd prefer me to directly bomb a hospital. He's a hypochondriac, you see. Reckons he's got every disease going. It's so bad he sometimes thinks he plays for Torino but, in actual fact, there's nothing wrong with him.

He'll sneeze and go: "I knew it. I've got pneumonia. Doctor..."

Or he'll spy a single spot and it's: "Told you, an allergic reaction to something I've eaten. Help, help, I'm dying. Doctor!"

Heaven forbid he gets an itchy nose. "No, not herpes, no! Doctor!"

It's a similar story out on the pitch. He'll mess up a shot, missing the target by miles, and all you'll hear is: "*Mamma mia*, must be the conjunctivitis to blame there."

At that point I'll intervene and try to calm him down. "You're absolutely fine, 100% healthy. Your only problem is you're a wanker."

He'll laugh, but that just brings on toothache. So he'll stop and his ears begin to burn. I know him, I like him and so I can't help fooling around. "Ale, you're losing blood from your nose."

"Must be an epistaxis!"

"An epi- what?"

"An epistaxis – a really small haemorrhage."

"It's a brain haemorrhage you've got…"

"A brain haemorrhage!!"

"I give up."

Any little twinge and he goes straight to the medics. If he thinks he's got the flu, he's checking his temperature every two seconds. It's reached the stage where I suspect he just likes using the thermometer, that it brings him some kind of pleasure. One night I was thinking about the whole thing and decided to play a joke. As soon as he'd gone off to sleep, I went and got a poster of Andrea Barzagli[57], one of those they give away with the *Hurrà Juventus* magazine, and pinned it up above his bed. I took a photo on my BlackBerry and sent it to a load of mates along with a three-word message: "Now that's love." A complete fabrication, of course. Precisely like all his ailments.

When he's in the bathroom brushing his teeth, shaving or making himself beautiful with all his lotions and potions, I'll burst in shrieking like a madman.

"What the fuck, Andrea? You'll give me a heart attack."

"Aaaaaand we're here again…"

He's a very anxious bloke, Matri, scared of everything. The doctor hates him. I adore him, just about as much as he loves Barzagli, because he has a priceless gift. Whenever he plays, all he needs is a single touch and he'll get you a goal. Let him have another touch and he'll score again. His strike rate is fantastic – he's a hugely underrated player. If I was a president, a guy like him would be right at the top of my wish list. He comes with a billion-year guarantee.

Every so often, I tell him what I think. "Ale, you could cause any defender in the Italian league a headache."

"A headache?"

"Don't worry: it's only a figure of speech."

One of these days I'm going to secretly film him and stick the video on YouTube – it would go viral overnight. But you could watch it only once before it self-destructs: in football, Paganini dies before he's even born[58]. There are no repeats in this game. The things that players do can't be wound back and watched in slow motion, and some terrible errors of judgment occur as a result. Using the helping hand of technology simply isn't allowed under the current rules.

Referees cop a lot of flak because those in charge are welded to traditions that are more stupid than they are old. Certain individuals don't want to go down the road of in-game replays, something that would solve at least 50% of the current problems, kill all the controversy stone dead and make our (professional) lives a lot less eventful.

Zidane was sent off for a headbutt on Marco Materazzi in the 2006 World Cup final. Everyone knows the ref, Horacio Elizondo, took that decision after his assistants saw the images on TV, even if they technically couldn't be influenced by them. Luckily for us, they weren't experts in lip reading[59].

In today's climate, having that external aid would be massive for match officials. Referees aren't robots; the law of averages tells you they're going to get things wrong occasionally. I've also never been able to understand how linesmen can watch the ball being struck and at the exact same time judge whether the player receiving it is in line with the others. Not even a four-eyed monster could manage that.

Saying 'no' to technology is like something out of a sporting Third World. All you'd need is a small screen where the fourth official stands. (Incidentally, I've always thought that 'fourth official' sounds like some kind of special agent rather than one of the referee's assistants). They'd be able to settle all the most difficult questions pretty much in real time. Was the ball over the line? Was that foul committed in the box or just outside? Offside – yes or no? In all of five seconds, some real dilemmas would be reduced to absolute certainty. The ref would still take care of all the more subjective stuff, like judging whether a tackle is a foul, because TV pictures can't give you a definitive verdict there.

I'd love to see a more modern football. But at the apex of the power pyramid, where brains wither and wallets matter, people hide behind tradition and try to keep things the way they've always been. They pretend they've forgotten we used to wear pointed studs and played with a ball that weighed a kilo. Back in those days, we didn't have TV cameras, either. I'm not saying that John Wayne should make a science fiction film, but Steven Spielberg would certainly be in a spot of bother if special effects didn't exist. For one thing, he couldn't be himself.

The next step is obligatory if we're to overcome a mindset that's now out of date and counter-productive. One that doesn't take account of the changes we've seen on pitch, but also in society in general. It's high time that football's ruling class stopped dozing in their armchairs. Even opening one eye would be enough, or maybe just a little bit of both. They don't understand that their antiquated way of thinking causes huge harm to referees. It leaves them utterly on their own and in the snipers' crosshairs. Things they don't notice in a split-second (and, as I say, they're human and imperfect), millions of people see on TV. The folks watching on think "He's fucked that one up: what a total idiot."

What they should really be thinking is: "Poor soul: he's being forced to operate in a bygone era."

You don't get black-and-white sets any more. But even just realising that TV has been invented would be a major step forward for certain people. It would also help those individuals who still obsess over pictures of the Sulley Muntari 'goal' that wasn't given in the now infamous Milan-Juventus match from 2012[60]. Perhaps they could finally let it go and delete the photos from their phones.

At the end of every game, more in Serie A than the Champions League, it has to be said, managers and directors line up to pass comment on the referee. They talk about what's not gone well; the mistakes that made them lose their cool. This painful vivisection of the game's most controversial moments goes on for hours and hours. They talk about the 'ideal decision' and compare it to the one taken on the pitch. It's always the same uncharitable message: the match officials got it wrong. Again. They're completely unreliable.

There should be more honesty in what people say. Players should remember the pass they misplaced; coaches the formation they messed up. Directors should recall the bad signings they've made, fans some of the songs they've sung, and Matri his medicine box. Passing judgment on others is always a lot of fun. Looking inwards is that little bit more difficult.

We need to get one thing straight. 'Let's throw ourselves into the future' can't just be an electoral slogan or an advert for a swimming pool in Nyon or Zurich. It needs to become a way of thinking, a real desire to change for the better. Other sports have taken that leap without suffering any negative repercussions.

Let's say Rafael Nadal's got match point at the Australian Open. The chair umpire decides the ball's in, awards an ace and gives Nadal victory. But Hawkeye, the electronic aid commonly used in tennis, says he's got it wrong. Truth is the winner: the match continues, Nadal goes off and serves again without complaint, his opponent doesn't mouth off ad infinitum, the umpire puts his hand up to say he got it wrong and the fans immediately forget the whole thing to concentrate on the next point. No losers and no controversy.

Either we start playing on a pitch made of blue cement or we use the available technology regardless of the tournament we're competing in. One or the other.

---

56 Striker Alessandro Matri played with Pirlo at Juventus before signing for Milan in 2013

57 The Juventus and Italy centre-back

58 Niccolò Paganini, perhaps the most celebrated violinist of all time, was thought to have died at the age of six but started moving again during his own funeral

59 Materazzi is alleged to have made insulting comments to Zidane about his mother and sister, provoking the Frenchman's angry reaction

60 In February 2012, Juventus and Milan were locked in a battle for the title. Milan took an early lead in the head-to-head at San Siro, and seemed to have doubled their lead when a shot from Sulley Muntari clearly crossed the line, only for the match officials to wave play on. Alessandro Matri equalised late on for Juventus, who went on to win the league by four points

Chapter 20

I know how to think. I'd hate it if people looked at me and fell into the trap of assuming: "Footballer. An EEG[61] on him wouldn't show much activity." There are, indeed, some pretty stupid players out there – I personally know a few of them. But then there are also surveyors, architects, teachers, musicians, journalists (I know a fair few), pharmacists and butchers with the same IQ as a rock.

Generally speaking, I reckon I'm a fairly switched-on guy. I've an opinion about everything and I'm not ashamed to express it, defend it and, where necessary, shout it from the rooftops. I can also tell when somebody's taking the piss out of me, or at the very least I'll have an inkling. If I don't have proof, I'll go with my gut feeling, like with a certain game in La Coruña back in 2004.

At the time I was playing for Milan, and we'd travelled to Spain to take on Deportivo in the second leg of a Champions League quarter-final. We'd won the first game 4-1 and the chances of us not going through were roughly equal to those of seeing Rino Gattuso complete an arts degree.

We were already thinking about the semis, as if we'd got it all sewn up even before we flew to Galicia. A tailor-made walk in the park. We hadn't taken into account a couple of possibilities. One, that the tailor might go mad and, two, that our own players could be struck down by collective amnesia. Every single one of them, all at the same time.

The impossible became reality. We forgot to play, and it ended 4-0 to them. They were laughing at us that night.

The first thing that needs to be said is that we did ourselves in. But, looking back with the benefit of hindsight, something doesn't stack up. Our opponents were going at a thousand miles an hour all night, even the older players who'd never exactly been known for their ability to combine speed with stamina.

What struck me most was how they kept on running at half-time. To a man: no exceptions. When the referee, Urs Meier, blew his whistle they all shot off down the tunnel as if they were Usain Bolt. They couldn't stand still even in that 15-minute period designed specifically to let you draw breath or at most just walk about.

We were chasing shadows all night. Their players were crazy buzz bombs flying around all over the place. I don't have any proof, so what follows isn't an accusation – I'd never allow myself to go that far. It's simply a nasty thought I've occasionally let percolate in the intervening years.

For the first and only time in my life, I've wondered if people I'd shared a pitch with might have been on something. Maybe it's all just anger that I haven't yet managed to work through. But the Deportivo players were like men possessed, galloping towards a target that only they could see. For our part, we were completely blind, and duly brutalised.

Whatever the truth of the matter, they came up against Porto in the semis and went out[62]. Within a short space of time, they'd disappeared from the face of all the major European competitions.

It does make me laugh, however, when people put the word 'doping' anywhere near the sacred name of Barcelona. They're an elite circle who pass their secret down from generation to generation. The recipe is simple: to win with minimum effort, you make the ball do the work. The masters of the Camp Nou know how to run, but you never see them undertaking 70- or 80-metre sprints. At most, it'll be 15 – they're always looking ahead and they never tire themselves out.

I imagine that drugs are a marginal problem in Italian football. We players are the subject of continual and extensive observation. We frequently, and gladly, receive visits from CONI[63] and UEFA representatives, who make us undergo surprise tests. Not just urine, mind – they also take our blood. They'll turn up during training, make themselves known and order us to follow them. They'll take us into the dressing room, gym or medical area, man-marking us as we provide our samples. No player ever complains, and rightly so. As far as we're concerned, transparent test tubes and honest syringes are always welcome.

It would be really stupid to take a banned substance, both because of the trouble it would cause your conscience and the fact you'd be found out straight away. At the start of each season, the club's medical staff give us a list of medicines we shouldn't use. I'll call the doctor even if I'm thinking about taking an aspirin – the danger of doing something irresponsible helps me stay ever vigilant. I'm like Matri in

145

this regard: doping's a disease I'll never catch and yet it scares the life out of me.

I get angry when cyclists give interviews and accuse footballers of being spoilt. Too rich, they say, always in the spotlight, total *prima donnas*. And yet they forget that ours is undoubtedly a clean world. The stuff that's coming out about theirs doesn't surprise me. Ex-riders admitting to using banned substances doesn't even make the headlines any more. People now take it as read that it's been a widespread practice for years. And that is truly sad.

It seems they're all at it, not least because for any normal person it would be impossible to pedal 300km a day, at maybe 40km per hour, then get up and do the same 24 hours later, and then once again the following day.

Events like the Tour de France, Giro d'Italia and Vuelta a España require riders to be at peak fitness for weeks on end. Some of those mountain climbs would melt a car engine, yet the cyclists manage to keep going. They've talked about legalising doping, but that strikes me as an obscenity – much better to shorten the stages.

It really annoyed me when Lance Armstrong, and thereafter a procession of support riders (or supporting actors…), admitted they'd deceived their opponents. That they'd whored themselves out to certain gurus just to get on the podium. It's not the confession that bothers me; that's the sacred part of this whole discussion. I'm more concerned with the hundreds of times they denied it, acting all indignant and threatening reprisals and lawsuits against those who were unmasking them. In the end, the authorities stripped Armstrong of seven Tour de France titles after showing that he'd scaled the Eiffel Tower in a helicopter.

Nothing to do with training. Zero titles won on the pitch, to coin a phrase ...

I just hope they teach the younger cyclists that it's wrong to cheat. Perhaps they need to take a piece of paper and write the names of everyone who already has. Or maybe it would be better to make a list of those who've gone too soon, having died in suspicious circumstances. That sort of shock treatment is certainly required. On cigarette packets you'll see 'smoking seriously endangers health' in big block capitals, and from that point on, it's completely the smoker's responsibility if they happen to get ill. Perhaps on bike frames we should now be writing: 'Don't put any shit in your water bottle.'

If I look in the mirror when I get up, or before going to bed at night, I see a man of average ugliness. With stubble, an unruly mane of hair, a squint nose, slightly protruding ears and bags under my eyes. But I also see a man who's completely happy with the figure staring back at him. Who's proud of every single second of his past.

Gino Bolsieri at Flero and Roberto Clerici at Voluntas weren't just the first coaches to understand that my ideal position is in front of the defence. Apart from my dad Luigi and mum Lidia, they were also the first people to remind me that taking a shortcut might help you finish first, but one day you'll find yourself face to face with your demons and you'll lose. You'll perish in a hell that you yourself helped create.

I do have something that burns inside me, an Olympic torch deep within. It's a violent fire, made of flames and passion and fed by pure pleasure. To put it out, to put *me* out, they'll need to douse my soul. Pretty much everyone who's been even half-listening knows what I'm talking about. As do the directors of Al-Sadd, the Qatari club who qualified for the 2011 FIFA Club World Cup.

When my agent Tinti rings and gets straight to the point without bothering to say hello, you know there's something serious going down. "Andrea, the guys from Qatar want you."

"Come again?"

"You're going to play in Qatar."

"Are you mad? I wouldn't dream of it."

"What are you saying?"

"I'm saying it's too soon."

My last season at Milan was on the home straight and I didn't have the slightest intention of emigrating.

"But even Guardiola played over there."

"Yes, at the end of his career."

"Okay then. But you need to go and meet them, just to be polite."

"Fine – when do they arrive?"

"They're already in Milan. Stick on a tie – I'll come and pick you up in an hour."

They were waiting for me at the Principe di Savoia, a fabulously luxurious hotel close to the main train station, where David Beckham stayed during his time at Milan. The Qataris had booked out an enormous suite and in it were the club's owner, a few directors and a swarm of lawyers.

"*Ciao*, your contract's ready."

"Good day to you as well; it's an honour to meet you ..."

"You'll look great in our strip."

"Pleasure to meet you, my name's Andrea Pirlo."

"You don't have to make up your mind straight away.

We'll give you a few minutes to think it over."

"In truth, I've only come here to find out who you are."

There was something of a linguistic incompatibility at work, a fissure in the space/time continuum. They were travelling in the future while I focused on the present. Even so, they made a good impression. That was the day I discovered that Father Christmas does exist.

"Andrea, how many kids have you got?" they asked.

"Two."

"Well, we've an excellent English language school in Qatar."

"I actually quite like hearing them speak Italian."

"No problem. We'll build a new one and employ only Italian teachers. Are you a fan of cars?"

"Yes ..."

"Great. We'd be delighted if you'd accept a few Ferraris as a gift."

"A few?"

"And if you find yourself missing Italy, there will always be a private jet sat on the runway for you."

"But ..."

"The contract's ready. It's for four years."

"Thanks but ..."

"It's for 40 million Euros."

At that point Tinti almost passed out.

"40 million over four years, not per season. You'll understand we can't go overboard, what with the financial crisis."

"Ah yes, I understand."

"But if 10 million a year isn't enough, don't worry, let's talk."

It was all too much. If I'd asked them to reclaim the desert, perhaps they would have said 'yes'. To avoid further temptation, I forced myself to end the chat.

"Many thanks, but I can't," I said. "Signing for you would mean signalling the end of my career, and I still think I've got a lot to give in Europe, in Italy. If I change my mind, I'll be in touch in a year or two."

"11 million."

"Tullio, let's go."

"Twelve."

"Tullio."

"Thirteen."

I had to basically drag away my agent, who was in a state of ecstasy. We made our escape. I looked at my watch and realised the time was 21:21. My favourite number, twice over. Destiny was whispering softly in my ear: "You did the right thing in there."

My dad was born on the 21st. It's also the day I got married and made my debut in Serie A. It became my shirt number early on and I've never let it go. It brings me luck, and that's the reason this book stops at 20 chapters. I like to think that the next one is made up of blank pages, waiting to be filled with other tales and experiences yet to be written.

And one thing's for sure – I've got a pen.

---

61 A scan to assess the brain's electrical activity

62 After a goalless draw in Portugal, Porto won the second leg 1-0 to reach the final, where they beat Monaco 3-0

63 The Italian Olympic Committee

Thanks

Thanks to Andrea Pirlo, first because I've found a friend. Secondly, because when he starts talking, there's no stopping him, and that's the discovery of the century.

To my wife Eleonora, who talks more about Andrea than me, but that's okay: she's the discovery of a lifetime.

To Cesare Prandelli, for a preface written from the heart and re-read the day of a game. He was thinking about the World Cup but he still found time to think of us.

To Martina Maestri, who read everything first up. She's the Pirlo of friendship.

To Daniele De Rossi, for his advice on the jokes and the messing around.

To Marco Nosotti and Veronica Baldaccini, for all the time they gifted me. They're my *Nazionale*.

To Massimo Ambrosini, for explaining Pirlo's character to me.

To Paola because, come on, there must be a library up there otherwise what kind of heaven would it be?

To all my Coverciano friends, in particular Simone Orati,

for pretending not to notice when I sneaked into secret rooms out of hours.

To Andrea Delmonte, for believing in me (and the man from Delmonte said 'yes').

To Ciacia Guzzetti, whom Samuel Eto'o called mum.

And, obviously, to my dad Mario and mum Carola, to my sister Benedetta, to my grandmother Sandra and my family in general. They're always the first names on my teamsheet. All of them.

Alessandro Alciato

Index

A

Stadio San Paolo 127
Stellini, Cristian 57

T

Tardelli, Marco 64-65
Tassotti, Mauro 74
Tempera, Vince 22
Terim, Fatih 79-81
Thiago Silva 74
Tinti, Tullio 2, 5, 18-21, 63,
65, 148-50
Torino FC 137
Totti, Francesco 35-36, 61, 109

U

Udinese FC 85-86
UEFA 72, 145

V

Van Bommel, Mark 5
Van Persie, Robin 72
Vatta, Sergio 39
Vespa, Bruno 78

W

World Cup Mexico 1986 39
World Cup Italia 1990 39
World Cup Germany 2006
12, 16, 18, 35, 40, 48, 71, 120
World Cup final (July 9, 2006)
12, 31-32, 139

World Cup South Africa 2010
46

X

Xavi 26, 70

Z

Zeman, Zdeněk 74
Zico 119
Zidane, Zinedine 139

Barça: The Making of the Greatest Team in the World

Football Book of the Year
– *British Sports Book Awards*

Book of the Year
– *Football Supporters'*
  Federation Awards

'A superbly written analysis
and celebration of Pep, Messi,
Xavi, etc. A brilliant book'
Henry Winter
The Daily Telegraph

'An instant classic'
Sports Illustrated

BackPage Press